Universal Scams & Fraud Detection

"In God we Trust"

*"If it sounds too good to be true,
it is too good to be true"*

DAVID SNOW

Acknowledgements

In writing this book, I would like to express my thanks and acknowledge the assistance from my editors Paul Fitzsimons and Shirley Sleator who worked tirelessly on editing the manuscript. Thank you to Chuck Whitlock for the inspiration to write this book, my wife Jacinta and my mother Mary who supported me throughout the process.

I also pay thanks to my many friends in the Irish Police force, An Garda Siochana, Una Dillon, Alan Perkins and Heather Millett of the International Association of Financial Crime Investigators (IAFCI) and my friends within various law enforcement agencies in the United States of America. Thanks also to Oliver Lindsiepe of the International Association of Special Investigation Units (IASIU), Rachel Fitzsimons and my many colleagues within Fraud Prevention. But most of all, I want to thank the victims of fraud who have shared their individual stories in the hope that others may benefit from the awareness of the scams. Most notably two very brave ladies and mothers of children on both sides of the heavenly divide, Ann Conroy and Fran Gibney.

First Published in 2014
Copyright 2014 David Snow

Published by Patriot Way
All rights reserved

ISBN: 1500547158
ISBN 13: 9781500547158

No part of this publication may be reproduced, stored in a retrieval system or transmitted; in any form or by any means, without the prior written permission of the Author, nor be otherwise circulated in any form of binding or cover other than that in which it is published and without a similar condition being imposed on the subsequent publisher.

The right of David Snow to be identified as the Author of the work has been asserted by him in accordance with the Copyright Design and Patents Act 1988.

A percentage of the sale of this book will be donated to A Little Lifetime Foundation www.isands.ie

Dedication

This book is dedicated to the bravery of Ann Conroy, Fran Gibney, Ron Smith Murphy, Leslie & Bobby Shaw, Mary Tallouzi, Jim Lygate and to all parents who have lost children of all ages.

I also remember my School friend Garda Gareth Harmon and his colleague Garda Conor Griffin and all Police Officers who have paid the ultimate price for protecting the innocent.

For my children
Kirsten, Andrew, Olivia & Sarah

Universal Scams & Fraud Detection

"In God we Trust"

Technical Fraud Management:
1. Introduction. 3
2. Why Criminals Commit Fraud. 9
3. A Fraud prevention model for a Financial Institution & The integrated elements of A Special Investigations Unit or Fraud Prevention Team 15
4. The Implementation of a European Multiple Country Fraud Strategy. 29
5. Cross Border Investigations. 37
6. How to recognise a Fraud Predator 47
7. Terrorist Financing By Fraud 57
8. Interview Techniques. 65
9. Surveillance 73

Universal Fraud & Scams:

10. Retail Fraud & Theft 81
11. Employee Theft: 89
12. Identity Theft 101
13. Insurance Fraud. 113
14. Banks, Credit Cards & Cybercrime 141
15. Car Scams 155
16. Fraud against the Elderly. 165
17. Internet Dating - Love Rats 173
18. Fraud Terminology General Terms 183

Epilogue. 191
About the Author 193

Technical Fraud Management – Prevention & Detection

{1}

Introduction

"Our prime purpose in this life is to help others. And if you can't help them, at least don't hurt them."

Dalai Lama

Crime comes in many forms as does the criminal. For decades society has been studying the effects of crime and criminals with the assistance of experts such as Criminologists and Psychologists. A particular area of crime that has fascinated me and others, for many years, is fraud. The Oxford English definition of the word fraud is *"wrongful or criminal deception intended to result in financial or personal gain."*

Indeed, you could spend the day surfing the internet looking at the many different definitions of the word fraud, which

Universal Scams & Fraud Detection

can also differ amongst financial institutions. The laws of our respective countries also have many legal variations defining fraud. However if you take the eight commandment of the Bible *"Thou shalt not steal"*, then, you will not go too far wrong.

Fraud is prevalent in all walks of life, from street-level crimes against the individual citizen to white collared criminals employed by corporations, some at the highest levels. Putting a global value on the cost of fraud is almost impossible. However, in a study carried out by the Association of Certified Fraud Examiners (ACFE), it was estimated that 5% of organisations' revenue is lost to fraud. When this is applied to the gross world product, annual potential fraud losses can be estimated at $3.5 trillion globally.

Financial Fraud is complex in its own right and comes in many forms affecting financial organisations and individuals. The investigation of fraud is difficult, time- consuming and costly. Fraud does not stop at country borders or state lines. It is a cross-border multi-jurisdictional phenomenon that cannot be stopped by a single entity or force. With this in mind, there is now, more then ever, a need for harmonisation of laws and law enforcement across, not only specific countries such as the United States of America, but also European, African and

Introduction

Asia-Pacific, Australian countries and continents. Perhaps it is easier to state that Fraud is a Global problem.

There is a bigger question at play which we, as honest citizens, individuals and business owners, generally do not think about and that is - just who exactly pays for the crime of fraud? There is a very simple answer to this question.

"You do!"

From the outset of this book, it is important to understand that fraud, in all its shapes and forms, is paid for by you, the consumer. We will examine and explore different types of fraud and financial crime or scamming, including insurance fraud, credit card fraud, identity theft, terrorist financing, retail crime and general scams.

For example, let's take Credit Card fraud. Most of us who have credit cards don't realise that the interest we pay on our card balances includes a sum to cover the lender's fraud losses.

The Insurance industry is also an easy area to see the cost of fraud. Most of us will have some form of insurance policy, on our car, our homes or travel insurance. Again, the cost of the premium paid to an insurance company includes a sum to

Universal Scams & Fraud Detection

cover fraud. It is estimated that in the United States Insurance fraud costs US$38,000…. every minute of every day.

For me personally, there is nothing lower on the criminal-fraud or financial-crime ladder then scamming an elderly citizen or any vulnerable person. We all have a duty to protect these people for their life-long contributions to society and to their families. We should assist the Police and fraud fighting professionals at every opportunity to prevent the con-artist from perpetrating their trade of fraud against all. But, in particular, the elderly and vulnerable.

In writing this book, I have very much aimed at entertaining the reader with the various stories of fraud and deception. I have either investigated or met with the investigators and Detectives behind these cases. However, I have also written the book to educate, in an effort to protect you, your home, family and your company from these conmen. From my personal experience in dealing with fraudsters, it never ceases to amaze me just how intelligent they can be and the lengths they will go to in order to succeed with their elaborate scams, fraud or other financial crime. As financial fraud is perceived by some to be "victimless", there can be a sense of respect towards these criminals by the general public. I find this most strange but understand that, in particular, defrauding financial institutions is seen as an achievement.

Introduction

Generally they are individuals who have an ability to tell lies without a second thought or conscience, enabling them to succeed in beating the system. Many large financial companies have recruited specialist fraud investigators and established Special Investigation Units (SIU's).

We will cover the recruitment of ideal anti-fraud personnel in another chapter. It should be said though, that these individuals are professional and are determined to succeed in detecting and preventing the con artists from succeeding.

So let us begin our journey, with a brief look at the history and reasons why individuals turn to crime, in particular fraud.

{2}

Why Criminals Commit Fraud

"He who commits injustice is ever made more wretched than he who suffers it."

Plato

Criminology is the legal science applied to the studying of crime. It gives an insight into the world of crime and the reasons why individuals choose to turn to the dark road of crime. I recently completed a Diploma in Criminology, studying under Professor John O'Keefe, the distinguished Criminologist. A Diploma in Criminology is effectively dipping your big toe into the study of Criminology, and I would highly recommend all investigators or fraud prevention staff complete such a course.

Universal Scams & Fraud Detection

There have been many thesis and studies by Criminologists into the reasons why people make the decision to turn to crime. These studies indicate that bad parenting, peer pressure in the teenager years, excitement, pure badness or simply being 'born bad' are the primary causes. However, when examining fraud and the reasons people turn to fraud, we need to take a look at the Fraud Triangle founded by noted American Criminologist Mr Donald Cressey. This triangle illustrates that, in order for fraud to be committed by an individual, the following three factors or elements must be present:

1 Pressure or Motivation
2 Opportunity
3 Rationalisation.

We will examine each of these elements in detail. I am of the view that Mr Cressey's Fraud Triangle has stood the test of time and can be applied to all types of fraud and financial crime including, in particular, white collar fraud by both an internal or external individual.

Fraud and financial crime prevention managers can learn much from the study of these three elements. The principle of any fraud-prevention strategy should be written using these elements, or at the very least, with them in mind.

Why Criminals Commit Fraud

DONALD CRESSEY'S FRAUD TRIANGLE

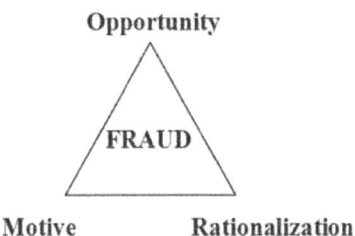

1 Pressure/Motivation: Individuals who are under financial stress or difficulty, perhaps because of the recession, loss of employment or addiction to narcotics, alcohol or gambling and need cash.

2. Rationalisation: A person may be of the view that they have an entitlement to the money. For example, with insurance fraud, the attitude in society might be "sure isn't everybody doing it?" The individual has convinced themselves that the criminal act is justified.

3. Opportunity: The individual sees the opportunity and calculates that there is a minimal risk of being caught. An example of a perceived victim may be a retail outlet without any security measures. This is where we, the potential victim, can protect ourselves. The drafting and implementing of security procedures, which should meet with compliance and governance standards will assist in the prevention of opportunistic crime.

OPPORTUNISTIC AND PREMEDITATED FRAUD

From my experience, I am of the view that individuals who commit fraud and financial crime do so because they are either opportunistic or premeditated. The Fraud triangle illustrates the elements or climate which needs to be present but there are two distinct types of individual who want to commit fraud.

An opportunistic individual is someone who is not necessarily bad or someone who plans to commit crime. It is an individual who effectively is in the right place at the right time, or the wrong place at the wrong time. Opportunistic criminals are ordinary individuals who decide to commit a crime. An example of this would be seeing somebody drop their wallet and waiting till they walked on before picking it up and pocketing the cash. Another example, one I have personally experienced in my work, would be somebody having a genuine insurance claim but embellishing the details to increase the value of the claim. One particular gentlemen told me that his 50 inch HD Sony plasma TV had been stolen from his house, when in fact it was a Sony 21" standard television. A normally genuine decent man who crossed the line because he saw the opportunity to make a few extra Dollars.

Why Criminals Commit Fraud

The second and more sinister conman is a Premeditating criminal. This is an individual who plans to commit the crime. Investigating premeditated fraud can be extremely difficult, depending on the expertise of the criminal and the lengths they are prepared to go to succeed and to avoid capture.

One example of premeditated fraud, involved an individual who filed a false insurance claim reporting that his Rolex watch had been stolen whilst he was in Los Angeles.

It is assumed that because they fraudulently report an incident outside of the country or state, they will get away with it.

Co-operation between Financial investigators who are members of associations such as the International Association of Financial Crime Investigators (www.iafci.org) and the International Association of Special Investigation Units (www.iasiu.org) regularly exchange information and training material.

In the case of the stolen watch, an investigator in Los Angeles found the Rolex watch for sale by a relative of the insured. When confronted with this information, the insured dropped his claim.

Universal Scams & Fraud Detection

Another example of premeditated fraud involved the reported theft, by a recession-hit individual, of his high-value car. Following an anonymous tip-off suggesting the claimant had himself left the car in an airport car-park, his claim was investigated. The electronic car keys, hold detailed information on the vehicle, including the date and time the key was last used and the mileage recorded on the vehicle. The date and time of the key report did not match that provided on the insurance claim form and statement of fact. The Specialist Police team, the Stolen Vehicle Unit, which is part of the National Bureau of Criminal Investigation, working with Dublin Airport Security personnel located the vehicle in the airport car park. They even got a nice image on CCTV of the insured collecting his car park ticket from the entrance barrier, while driving the "stolen car". The man was prosecuted for deception receiving a suspended jail sentence.

OPPORTUNITY AND INCLINATION RESISTANCE

Finally, it's the above *equation* that will make the difference. The resistance is not just law enforcement and fraud investigators, but also the general public who can assist in the prevention of fraud. Together, we are the resistance.

{3}

A Fraud prevention model for a Financial Institution & The integrated elements of A Special Investigations Unit or Fraud Prevention Team

"Fail to Plan and Plan to Fail"
Benjamin Franklin

The implementation and management of a fraud model or strategy is now embodied in the business model of any progressive financial risk-based company. The modern day Special Investigations Unit (SIU) has evolved substantially over the past decade. Gone are the days of employing a

Universal Scams & Fraud Detection

single person to investigate and combat fraud. Most SIU teams consist of highly trained investigators, backed up by lawyers, analysts and IT support staff. In this chapter, we will examine what is needed to develop, manage and organise a financial crime prevention team or Special Investigation Unit, for the purpose of building a fraud prevention strategy.

Before taking a closer look at the requirements of the successful SIU team, I must emphasis that management input is critical to the objectives and approach to combating fraudulent attempts against a company. An adopted approach of *"we have a zero tolerance approach to those seeking to defraud us"* must have the backing of management at all levels and have the full support of the organisation at large. We are witnessing an increase in the amount of savings achieved by actively tackling fraud. This comes from the implementation of an effective fraud model fully embedded in the procedures of the Special Investigation Unit. The overall objectives or goals are to reduce risk to the business and to mitigate losses from fraud.

The development of a Fraud Prevention model should include the following key points and embrace suggestions and ideas from all departments within the organisation. International companies should also seek information and inspiration from outside the country as this will enhance the knowledge-base of the company's SIU and give a best practice approach to dealing with fraud. It is critical to obtain staff buy-in which should be achieved not just with financial incentive for success but also with executive praise for successful criminal prosecutions.

Fraud Prevention Model – Key Considerations:

- Create a culture of fraud awareness in everything your staff do
- Embrace effective and empowered Fraud Leadership
- Create a universal fraud identification program
- Create effective IT platforms to support ground level activity and accurate Management Information (MI) production
- Data mine on all held data and available external data sources
- Increase strategic profile of fraud prevention within the specific industry
- Become Thought Leaders
- Offer full support to all staff
- **Never stop learning from fraudsters**

Special Investigators

There will always be the requirement to employ professional investigators with good detection skills for the investigation of fraud, such as suspect financial transactions, attempts to obtain credit or indeed insurance claims. In the financial sector, these individuals are typically former law enforcement personnel who possess expert knowledge and experience for investigating potential financial crime. However, when employing investigators, organisations should not limit the selection to former law enforcement officers. There are also excellent financial investigators from other disciplines, such as former Private Investigators, Insurance Claim Handlers, Loss Adjusters, Bank Staff and Military personnel. At the core of an SIU is the professional dedicated investigator who has the ability and will to work long and flexible hours. Consideration should also be given to the investigators' areas of expertise. Investigators typically operate within a geographic location, but it would be more beneficial for investigators to be used for different types of investigation, based on experience. This is not always possible due to manpower restrictions and the geographic location of an investigation.

The key attributes a financial investigator should possess are dedication, openness to possibilities and, above all, attention to detail with the ability to obtain evidence that will stand up to legal scrutiny and cross examination in a court of law.

Outsourcing / Contracted Investigators

Irrespective of budget restrictions for investigation, there will always be a need to call on expertise from outside the SIU operation in areas such as surveillance, tracing of witnesses, forensic accounting or fire investigation. In many jurisdictions including Ireland and the UK, there is no legal requirement to obtain a license to operate as a Private Investigator. It would be prudent to consider identifying high-calibre quality investigators and surveillance agents to support combating fraud. The selected outsourced investigators should then be tied into a contract to include a Service Level Agreement, which will maintain quality and cost control. In addition, regular detailed audits should be carried out on the contracted investigators.

The Financial Fraud Manager:

The SIU or Fraud Manager should be a strong-willed and dedicated individual who is firm but fair with the team. As the leader of the SIU they will pull the team together and obtain the best from each assigned individual member. We all have strengths and weaknesses, it is the responsibility of the manager to identify candidates best suited, to maximise the effectiveness of the combined team. If the individuals assigned are contributing to a successful SIU, this will reflect positively on the overall organisation.

Universal Scams & Fraud Detection

The Fraud Manager should instigate the development of a database of central investigation control. This database should be available for all staff and contracted service providers such as Lawyers or support staff. The database should include a file identification number, the name and address of the individual being investigated, the financial implication, details of the circumstances of risk and the suggestions or reasons for the referral to the SIU. The investigators will use the database to manage their workload, input investigation results and report any financial savings. The organisation's IT department should assist with the development of the database. This database should feature a metric filtering option for automatic referral, filtered by red-flag items and other mined data.

The example below is a database design for an insurance company, but could be designed to include referrals for any SIU team working within financial fraud investigation.

Sources of Investigation Referrals

Having a centrally-controlled database is crucial, as it will facilitate the monitoring of referrals between departments or by line specific area of business. It should also allow for the tailoring to the specific needs of the Fraud Manager and consideration should be given to ongoing performance reviews of both internal and contracted investigators. The database itself should be analysed to provide accurate management information on a monthly basis, so as to measure and inform management on the level of financial crime prevention, detection and overall effectiveness of the Special Investigations Unit.

TRAINING..... ONE OF THE KEYS TO SUCCESS

All staff within an organisation should receive fraud awareness training. One of the most important functions of an SIU is to provide this training. Moreover it should not be limited to SIU staff. Fraud awareness training should be provided to all internal personnel and also include contractors and service providers. This training should be accredited to a recognised and accepted industry standard. It should be continuous and a minimum of a refresher or updated training course should be given to all employees once a year.

There is also a need to provide suitable advanced training for the SIU investigation team. This training can be achieved by attending fraud workshops and seminars, which are provided in America, Europe and the Asia Pacific region by the International Association of Financial Crime Investigators (www.iafci.org) or the International Association of Special Investigation Units (www.iasiu.org). There are also excellent books available to investigators such as *Conquering Deception by Jeff Nance* and *Scam School by Chuck Whitlock*, both available on Amazon, or *SIU Today* available from IASIU. Training for experienced investigators is best achieved by word of mouth, sharing stories and experiences with each other through various channels and workgroups.

SUCCESS WILL BE ACHIEVED BY WORKING TOGETHER (IN CLOCKWORK MOTION)

LEGAL SUPPORT

As we now live in an increasingly litigious society, consideration should be given to retaining the expertise of a lawyer who specialises in the defence of litigation and prosecution of crime, either as an employee or on a contract basis. It is the duty and objective of the investigators to gather the facts of the case and the surrounding circumstances. These reports need to be examined by a legal professional who has the knowledge and ability to give legal advice to the investigators and to effectively manage the case. This has proved to be an effective method in the investigation of suspect insurance claims and the referral of potential criminal files to law enforcement agencies.

IT Support Systems – Data Mining

The essence of a fraud prevention strategy is to prevent fraud by the identification of suspect transactions or activities which, after intervention and / or investigation, prove to be of a fraudulent nature. The investigation unit of any financial institution has limited resources so it is therefore crucial to have in place a filtering system, based on red flags or other metric-based analysis which filters suspect transactions to the investigation team. There are many IT companies offering the latest 'Silver Bullet' system which will stop fraud. The services these providers offer may be of benefit to you, but it is imperative that the supplier you choose, is specifically suited to your needs. For example the IT system needs to work in tandem with your current databases and customer transaction system. It is essential that the selected fraud system is compatible with the internal database software system in place. There also needs to be full support from both the supplier and the internal IT department. A partnership approach is required to fulfil the requirements which will then constantly evolve as perpetrators develop new methods of beating the system. It is also important that the combined IT team have a full understanding of financial fraud and the objectives of the organisation's fraud strategy.

POLICE LIAISON

Ireland's police force, An Garda Siochana, has a specialised unit, the Garda Bureau of Fraud Investigation (GBFI). Under various criminal legislation the GBFI provides a support and guidance service along with the investigation and prosecution of individuals. The Criminal Justice Theft and Fraud Offences Act 2001, covers a large amount of financial criminal legislation. Section 6 of the act "Making a gain or causing loss by deception" covers insurance fraud.

How a file is prepared for referral to the GBFI is crucial. The GBFI assessment unit require an official complaint as well as a fully detailed report. Preserved evidence is required and therefore, knowledge of the rules of evidence in criminal courts is important. As we are dealing with fraud, the majority of evidence in fraud cases will be documents. It is important to retain original documents which will be used as evidence exhibits in court. I have always found GBFI detectives willing to offer advice and guidance on fraud and other criminal investigation matters.

Most countries in the developed world have a national or local Police force with a specialist fraud investigation unit.

Universal Scams & Fraud Detection

The Federal Bureau of Investigation (FBI) in the United States and the British Police have trained specialists to assist in the investigation of fraud against individuals or companies. An individual who suspects that they are a victim of fraud should immediately contact the authorities. A department within a financial organisation who suspects fraud should contact the organisation's SIU or Security Manager.

Marketing & Industry Groups:

The Special Investigation Unit should be encouraged by senior management, to promote its operations and effectiveness to customers and staff, asking them to alert the organisation to any suspicions of fraud. The majority of successful investigations resulting in a discovery of fraud originate from a member of staff or the general public raising the alarm.

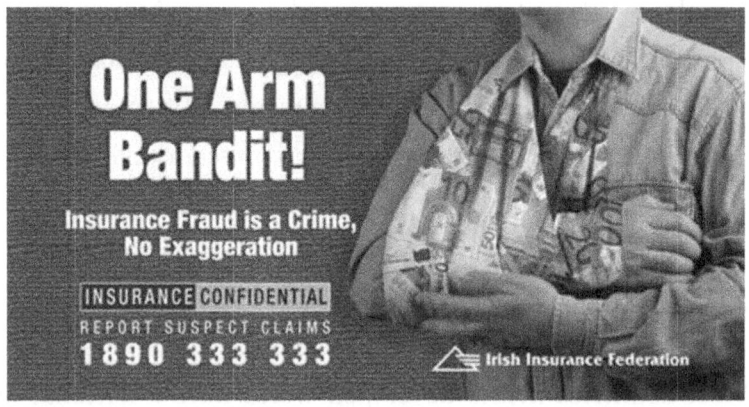

Sample Advertisement by the Insurance Ireland fraud forum

The Fraud Prevention Manager must take ownership of selling the SIU to all personnel within the organisation in order to maximise the effectiveness of the unit. At an industry level, it is also important to liaise with the media, sharing examples of successful cases. This can be achieved by either the Fraud Manager working with the organisations' marketing department or alternatively an industry fraud prevention group. An example of successful cases can be viewed at www.insurance-confidential.ie or http://www.insurancefraud.org/ or http://www.insurancefraudbureau.org/

Publicising successfully investigated cases may result in an opportunistic fraudster, deciding against committing their crime.

It is important that Fraud Prevention Managers from different organisations network, either informally or in an established networking group and meet on a regular basis to discuss tactics and to share knowledge and experience of recent successes and of local and international fraud trends.

In Summary the Fraud Prevention model at the core of an effective Special Investigation Unit will perform at its

Universal Scams & Fraud Detection

optimum, when it has the support of the SIU's staff and company personnel at large as well as the backing of management. The success will be measured in financial savings from the detection and prevention of fraudulent activity against the organisation.

{4}

The Implementation of a European Multiple Country Fraud Strategy

"Honest differences are often a healthy sign of progress."
Mahatma Gandhi

The management of fraud prevention in any one city, country or state is a complex issue and requires a clear and focused strategy. Managing fraud on a multi-country basis, particularly within the continent of Europe, is more complex and tedious. Over the past one hundred years, Europe has been fragmented by two horrendous world wars.

Universal Scams & Fraud Detection

Today, we find a united continent, with a single currency and governments unified through the common policies of the European Union. Despite this unity, Europe remains diverse in many ways, with numerous religions, ethnic backgrounds, languages, customs and laws. It is these many differences and history between the countries or member states that gives the continent its attraction to non-European tourists.

Therefore, when commencing an exercise of managing Fraud prevention solutions for any large multi-national company in the European region, it is important to embrace all cultural, social and economic diversities and to respect that difference is not wrong or a negative. The key to operating in a multinational organisation is studying the diversities of the different nations, identifying and utilising their strengths.

The first or second spoken language in most European countries is English. Therefore when designing a European or international fraud prevention strategy, just like Airline Pilots, English needs to be the chosen language.

In the financial sector, countries such as the UK, USA and to a lesser extent, Ireland have strong industry associations which effectively unite the individual financial organisations with the common goal of fraud prevention. Bodies such as the UK's CIFAS, Insurance Fraud Bureau and the USA's National Insurance Crime Bureau compile and provide comprehensive national fraud statistics and offer fraud prevention support to organisations. As a Regional Head of Fraud it is important to identify these institutions and to have regular meetings with them in order to support and maintain an understating of the local, national and regional fraud issues.

The International Association of Financial Crime Investigators and Special Investigation Units are the most widely-recognised international fraud-prevention bodies. They offer global support to insurance companies and other financial institutions, along with country specific investigators.

Members of IAFCI and IASIU can attend the European and American conferences which provide invaluable experience, knowledge and insight to assist in combating financial fraud across jurisdictions. It is interesting to learn that insurance or credit card fraud in South Africa, Germany, UK, USA or Australia is similar.

Fraud against financial institutions are either crimes of opportunity by an individual or perpetrated by those involved in organised crime. Knowing this makes it easier to design an effective fraud prevention strategy. Fraud is fraud, no matter in what country you reside. Its each countries' laws, customs and interpretation of the fraud that differ.

MULTIPLE JURISDICTION FRAUD MANAGEMENT STRATEGY

Step One Gain local knowledge of local SIU / management, fraud issues	**Step Two** Understand country strategy & develop, examine high priority areas for fraud
Step Three Establish FTE and IT needs, use matrix to build on success for incremental financial benefit	**Step Four** Develop training materials and recognition for local investigators. Provide support to management

The cross-jurisdiction European fraud-prevention strategy, should reflect the strategies of the individual companies and countries involved. Once it has been designed, confirmed and brought into effect by all concerned, the strategy must be

The Implementation of a European Multiple...

implemented. Consideration should also be given to the overall Global strategy of the organisation.

The process should also include an introduction to the local Management team and, if possible, the organisation's local Chief Executive Officer.

Combating financial fraud must be filtered from the top down to all levels within the organisation. By securing the respect and support of all involved on a local, national and regional level, only then is it possible to influence legal and law enforcement communities within the country of operation. It is also vital to think universally, to keep the entire region in mind when implementing the strategy - a process applicable to one region, country or organisation may also be suitable for another - or, equally importantly, might *not* be suitable for another. An example of this could be a potential idea, for example in Austria could be of benefit in Italy, or vice versa.

It is important to get an understanding of the relevant industries within a jurisdiction and the organisations within those industries. Coordinating the efforts of the fraud teams through an industry body is also important as attending these meetings gives an understanding of the local industry concerns and issues.

Universal Scams & Fraud Detection

As we now live in the digital age of smart phones, tablets and Linkedin, we need to fully embrace technology to optimise communication. The ability to tele and video-conference and the ease with which information can be digitally shared is vital to any industry in the twenty-first century and none more important than fraud prevention.

It is equally important to have face-to-face, press the flesh meetings. It can be frustrating to spend two hours on a general conference call, listening to issues which, as important as they are, do not apply to your organisation or jurisdiction. A tele-or video conference call should be regarded as a formal meeting with an agenda and recorded minutes. It is also important that senior management personnel facilitate, encourage and attend regular face-to-face meetings amongst the community.

The fundamentals of management of people should be applied. Although the team may be spread out in various country locations, there is still a need to motivate and to provide strong emphasis on teamwork. This can be achieved by following the pointers below:
- Respect views and acknowledge good work
- Communicate honestly and openly. Be open to suggestions from all individuals and organisations.
- Listen to the individuals and your team at all times, even when they have made an error.

The Implementation of a European Multiple...

- Be diligent and patient when recruiting and identify the most suitable individual for every position.
- Monitor the performance of individuals and teams.

Training is key to the success of any fraud-prevention strategy. There is a requirement for all fraud-prevention personnel to hold specific certification, which requires continued professional development to pre-determined standards. The development of fraud-prevention training material should be the responsibility of each jurisdiction and its senior personnel. Regional management should then co-ordinate a mechanism by which each jurisdiction shares its training procedures with others in the region, hereby creating a uniform training strategy across the industry. Despite the possible cultural and language issues across a region such as Europe, it should still be possible to apply the broad stokes of the strategy to most, if not all, organisations within the community. In addition, other jurisdictions, such as the Americas and Australasia, might be in a position to share their anti-fraud training strategies, creating a wider-spreading, possibly global, methodology.

Another area for consideration is unity. A multinational organisation with fraud-prevention departments in each jurisdiction, for example, should ensure that its anti-fraud departments are well connected and in full communication with each other.

Universal Scams & Fraud Detection

This can be achieved through internal training seminars and workshops. Outlining company SIU structure, methodologies, team personnel profiles and successful cases.

{5}

Cross Border Investigations

"We Never Sleep"

Allan Pinkerton

Looking back at the history of cross border criminal investigations and in particular the nineteenth-century North American Wild West, we see that prior to the establishment of interstate / multistate investigation agencies such as the FBI, infamous characters like Butch Cassidy and the Sundance Kid having robbed railroads and banks in Kansas, crossed the state border into Missouri. The local town Sheriffs were left powerless to pursue these individuals. That was until Allan Pinkerton decided to establish Pinkerton's National Detective Agency with the commitment that his pursuit of the outlaws did not stop at any state line. Pinkerton was also the inventor

Universal Scams & Fraud Detection

of what became known as *"The Wanted Poster"*, which we have become accustomed to in many Western cowboy movies. It was Pinkerton's trade mark or motto of *"We never sleep"* which suggested that Pinkerton and his Agents would never give up the pursuit of the outlaws, which put fear into the hearts of the frontier criminals of America in the 1880's. In effect, this motto meant that Pinkerton would never stop his pursuit of the outlaws.

The true life characters of Butch Cassidy and the Sundance Kid.

Today the European Criminal Intelligence Agency, Europol, advises that there are as many as three thousand organised

Cross Border Investigations

crime gangs perpetrating crime in operations across the European Union. These gangs are involved in the trafficking of people and drugs, financial crime, smuggling and terrorism. Europol working with the Irish Police have identified nine Irish criminal gangs operating across Europe, mainly in Holland, the UK and Spain. It's not the just the Irish gangs that Europol are targeting, they are also investigating Russian money laundering in the EU with investigations in Bulgaria, Cyprus, Latvia and Switzerland.

Cybercrime by its nature, like the internet, is borderless, which makes it difficult for law enforcement to investigate. Organised criminals and state sponsored cybercrime is growing and a significant problem. This is of significant concern for the United States and organisations, who are investing in advanced IT security. The British Secret Service MI5 advised that state sponsored Cybercrime has targeted UK industry with one major London listed company reporting losses of £800m as a result of a cyber attack.

The fraudster or conman does not necessarily stop at an international border. He continues to ply his trade of crime, conning individuals or organisations and institutions. As mentioned earlier in the introduction to this book, there is a real need for financial investigators to have the ability to investigate beyond the border of their individual country.

Universal Scams & Fraud Detection

The area of cross border or international investigations should be of interest to all senior national fraud prevention managers. It is imperative that fraud investigators in different countries and jurisdictions work with and support each other to prevent international financial crime. From my personal experience, the ability to call on a fellow investigator in a foreign country is important. Speaking from experience and having completed a successful major cross border investigation involving fraud investigation teams in the UK, Poland, Germany, Texas, Oklahoma, New Mexico and Colorado, I found it to be exciting. If marketed correctly, cross border co-operation in investigations of this magnitude can be used to sell the success of the fraud function and strategy.

All cross border investigations, large or small should be reported by the national fraud manager to the regional head of fraud. If the investigation moves out of the continent, it is important to then get the assistance and direction from the Global Head of Fraud. When executing cross-border investigations, having a single point-of-contact in each country involved will minimise confusion and enable a successful and expeditious result, and permits a better overall outcome of the investigation.

Cross Border Investigations

CHALLENGES OF CONDUCTING CROSS BORDER INVESTIGATIONS

Surveys among the fraud-prevention community have shown that there are many challenges associated with a cross border investigation:

Many of the surveys carried out provided interesting results. Consideration needs to be given to the following concerns:

(A) Lack of international resources for investigations*
(B) Lack of investigation confidentiality*
(C) Lack of co-operation from other departments within an organisation*
(D) Cultural differences
(E) Lack of reliable electronic communication email etc., access to the internet
(F) Danger to the investigators. Investigators personal safety is a must
(G) Language barriers / lack of translation services

The first three pointers above, highlighted with an *, should not be of concern to any well-managed Special Investigation Unit within a supporting organisation.

It is necessary to have good local and national experience within any investigation. To a well managed and coordinated global company with individual country fraud SIU's, in my experience it is always an advantage to have internal expertise at country level,. However having the ability to call on fellow IAFCI or IASIU members in specific countries is also most advantageous. A single point of contact (SPOC) in each country or jurisdiction is also of paramount importance. Some of the larger countries such as the UK or USA will have a multiple of fraud investigators in the Special Investigation Unit. An investigator should not have to explain a case or go through an update more than once. Therefore, having that single point of contact with fluency in the accepted common language will enable easy communication of intelligence. There is nothing more annoying and time consuming for an investigator having to explain the case and request assistance more then once to a number of different individuals. A single point of contact, who is fluent in English will make the investigation and passing of findings or intelligence much easier. It can also be embarrassing to organise a fraud conference call between multiple jurisdictions/countries regarding a specific case, and to have the attendance of an individual who is not familiar with or handling the investigation within a particular country.

THE MAIN ADVANTAGES OF PLANNED AND MANAGED CROSS BORDER INVESTIGATIONS ARE:

- It reduces the occurrence of Fraud against the organisation on a global scale

Cross Border Investigations

- It demonstrates to shareholders that the company has a positive attitude to combating fraud and financial crime
- It makes your company more competitive on an International level
- It helps develop a positive reputation of the organisation both within the company and with law- enforcement communities / agencies
- It generates positive publicity and improves the organisations general reputation.
- It raises individual and departmental morale and creates a sense of community within the global organisation

OUTSOURCED CROSS BORDER INVESTIGATORS

Hazards may arise on retaining the services of a Private Investigator in a country where your organisation does not operate and it is essential that you are aware of such hazards. In many of the European countries there is no licensing authority, training requirements or minimum competency level for any Private Investigators to meet. By not exercising due diligence when sourcing an investigator, we run the risk of employing one with inadequate skills and experience, who will do more harm to an investigation than good. By simply searching on the internet for a Private Investigator or Surveillance provider could provide you with an unprofessional operator with zero skills or qualifications as an investigator. Once again organisations such as IAFCI, IASIU or the World Association of Detectives (www.wad.net) can provide you with lists of Private Investigators who operate within the specific jurisdiction. As when retaining any service supplier, it is prudent to check with reputable referees. It is also advisable to obtain a written quote from any potential service provider prior to commencing a relationship.

Evidence:

The purpose of all investigations, including cross border investigations, is to obtain credible intelligence and evidence which may be of benefit to your investigation. It is important to remember that evidence obtained in a foreign country may not be admissible in the courts of your jurisdiction or other jurisdictions' courts of law. Before attempting to use the evidence, legal advice should be obtained from a member of the legal profession / lawyer. Whilst the burden of proof needed for a criminal conviction is significantly higher than a civil case, the presented evidence will need to stand up to scrutiny by vigilant lawyers within the court. It is also equally important to be aware of the costs involved in having the investigator travel from the country in which the evidence was obtained, to the country in which the court case will take place. I have experience of an Irish court case, in which evidence was obtained in California, and the court case was in Ireland. Much of the cost was travel-related and, as it transpired in this particular

Cross Border Investigations

case, unnecessary, as the investigator was not required to give evidence.

The cost of the investigator travelling to Ireland, including his personal fee was rather large. In the end it was not required to have the investigator attend. Thankfully with the development of the internet and email, video and photographic evidence can be viewed easily almost in any country of the world. However, for the provision of evidence, it is still a requirement to have the investigator in the court.

In summary when conducting a multi jurisdiction or cross-border investigation, an investigator should follow this process:

Universal Scams & Fraud Detection

LESSONS LEARNED

The following key points should be followed:
- ✓ Confirm the identity of the subject of the investigation
- ✓ Interview all witnesses available
- ✓ Inspect the location of the incident and take photographs
- ✓ Confirm ownership of any Motor Vehicle
- ✓ Establish if the subject/witness is in any employment
- ✓ Obtain a photograph or description of the subject of investigation
- ✓ Provide full information on your request to the selected investigator in the specific country
- ✓ Conduct internet intelligence research on the subject
- ✓ On a cross jurisdictional / multiple country investigation, have a single point of referral in each country and maintain control of the investigation
- ✓ Monitor the costs of the investigation and request formal written reports and evidence

{6}

How to recognise a Fraud Predator

"I'm a con artist in that I'm an actor. I make people believe something is real when they know perfectly well it isn't."
— John Lithgow

If I could offer guidance on how to identity a fraud predator before he or she strikes, then I would be a very wealthy individual. I have been working in the investigation and security industry for a quarter of a century. During that time, I have experienced many con-artists at work applying their evil cunning deceptive trades against retailers, individuals and corporate bodies. From basic retail shoplifting to complex identity theft, credit card scams and insurance fraud, these con-artists are intelligent and manipulative. These fraudsters display certain

Universal Scams & Fraud Detection

characteristics - confidence and a determination to succeed. These entrepreneurial characteristics makes it difficult for both organisations and individuals to protect themselves.

Before we look at how to recognise a con-man we should first look at the definition. If you Google the definition, the return is: *"a man who cheats or tricks someone by means of a confidence trick."* This is a straight forward definition as it's simple and easy to understand. The slang word 'con' is in fact derived from the word confidence.

In effect, a fraudster uses deception to obtain the confidence of an individual or organisation, to gain information which will benefit the fraudster and cost the victim, usually financially.

It is only by gaining knowledge and experience, reading books such as *Chuck Whitlock's Scam School*, (published by Macmillan) and by learning methods from the con artists themselves, that individuals and organisations will learn how to protect themselves. It is, by far, more cost effective and rewarding to prevent rather than detect the con artist. Take, for example, a bank offering credit facilities to a potential criminal or a retailer offering a store credit card. Before the fraud is detected the con artist may have already made off with a large financial sum. Being able to recognise an attempted

How to recognise a Fraud Predator

fraud before it happens is difficult but, by employing effective procedures and enabling well trained staff, it becomes a possibility. By detecting potential fraud using predictive analyses tools, ideally at application stage through application enrichment, or looking deeper at what lies behind the provided information, an organisation could save thousands of Euro. It is less costly to avoid the fraud than trying to manage it out of your organisation profits.

Typically, financial institutions use analytics before accepting an individual or organisation as a customer. An industry has grown from the need to provide such services and there are many quality companies operating in this arena. For example Risk Intelligence, part of the Moneymate Group, provide a solution for financial institutions operating across Ireland and Europe. Using advanced systems, they look behind the data that is being provided by applicants. This process is known as "quotation enrichment". Using complex data examination and applied weighting metrics, they are effectively predicting the level of risk associated with accepting an applicant to the financial institution. This process takes place in real time, while the applicant is inputting the data.

There is also a need to identify if the risk associated with the criteria of application has a prior history of fraud and or application abuse. An example of this would be a vehicle, insured by an insurance company, that has been previously written off. A case I investigated involved an individual who claimed that he crashed his truck into a wall. The accident happened only a week after he took out the insurance policy. However the Motor Assessor who inspected the vehicle was concerned that the damage was older than a week, as claimed by the insured. A check with Risk Intelligence, via the UK's Motor Industry Anti Fraud theft Register (MIAFTR), revealed that the vehicle had been involved in a serious road traffic accident and written off by a UK insurance company. I was in a position to obtain photographs of the damaged vehicle from the UK which confirmed that the damage was the same. When this was put to the customer by the Irish Police he confessed and also revealed that he had successfully perpetrated this con on two previous occasions. It was a case of third-time-unlucky. As a result of this case and others, insurance companies now run a Risk Intelligence check on all vehicles at quotation stage.

An identity thief trying to obtain a credit card from a bank, may be deterred if the bank has a tightly controlled and policed application procedures in place. Procedures, along with staff trained to recognise the illusive behaviour of applicants avoiding answers to simple questions, should prevent the issuing of the credit cards.

How to recognise a Fraud Predator

Unfortunately with pressures from senior management and shareholders, in today's modern society, fraud avoidance is sometimes skipped and Anti Money laundering checks are seen as an obstacle rather than an advantage to protect the company.

The professional con artist is aware of this and is skilled in getting around the basic anti-fraud questions most financial organisations ask. The charming, excessively friendly and even openly flirtatious tactics they use are designed to disarm bank personnel. Staff need to be trained to observe suspect conversational tones, body language and eye contact. It is important for the staff members to be aware that the only goal of the con artist is to get out of the branch or off the phone, having successfully gained credit.

The points below are my personal observations, having carried out many interviews of potential and convicted fraudsters:

- **Body language:** Watch for avoidance of prolonged eye contact and reduced blinking movements, both of which suggests dishonesty. Other indicators include excessive hand movements and touching of the face or mouth.
- **Charm:** The con-artist may use charm and flattery in cutting through any alertness or suspiciousness of the loan officer. Simple physical contact, as well as flattery such as "wow your hair looks beautiful" or "would you like to have dinner with me" are ploys used by the con artist. Effectively

the conman will play on emotions, ego and insecurities and tell you what you want to hear.

- **Pressure:** The con-artist will try to put a loan-officer under pressure to make a quick decision, using examples such as another customer about to buy the desired car or even a sick child at home needing regular transportation to hospital.
- **Confident:** A professional con-artist will be confident and assertive in their conversation and demeanour. He will study and research his victim and the details of his scam, just as a bank robber surveys a bank. For example a con-artist, when filing a false insurance claim, will research the phraseology and methodology used by the insurance industry.
- **Boasting:** In order to secure that credit card, a con-artist will talk about past successes in business and debt-repayment, all of which will be lies.

Note - Having had conversations with convicted con artists, they enjoy boasting about their success, and of having defeated security systems and corporate bodies.

Professional fraudsters are skilled in using conversation to extract details so as to exploit vulnerabilities. For example, discovering that a person lives alone allows a con-artist to take advantage of that person's loneliness.

How to recognise a Fraud Predator

If during a conversation with a person whom you think maybe a con artist, you should call for a colleague or a friend to assist you. If this is a genuine person they will continue the conversation, however most conmen will make an excuse and leave.

It is important not to let the suspected con-artist control the conversation. By remaining professional and courteous, but distant, the loan officer prevents the con-artist from taking advantage. The fraudster will try to play on your emotions, do not let them succeed.

One noticeable characteristic of a con-artist is their ability to tell lie after lie. Con-artists have told me that, in fact, their life becomes a lie and one of the hardest tasks for the conman is "keeping up with the lie". This will include promising the world, saying whatever needs to be said and talking convincingly about a subject he actually knows very little about. Most conmen may have little or no knowledge of the current topic of conversation but just enough to skim over the conversation and to convince or obtain the confidence of the individual. It is important to remember that a conman is simply looking to con you of your confidence.

A large part of being a con-artist is appearance and I have noticed that most con-men and women are, or make themselves, attractive and well-dressed. A well-cut suit or a sexy

Universal Scams & Fraud Detection

dress might be the key prop to gain the confidence of an individual, bank manager or company CEO, a thin but effective veneer covering a lack of substance, a little like a fancy book cover with a poor content. There is also a need to be wary of the individual who looking for personal information, wants to close the deal fast, speeding up the process for getting the money or credit card.

One example of this was an individual who secured a payment of a couple of thousand from an insurance company. He manufactured a false company identification card and obtained utility bills in the name of the person to whom the Insurance company cheque was made payable. He was able to open a bank account in that person's name and secure an overdraft facility. Following the bank's loss and subsequent investigation, it became apparent that the bank employee had been conned or convinced that the individual was an employee of the insurance company and that this was a monthly salary cheque. The bank employee was astounded that he had been conned by such a well - mannered and smartly dressed gentleman.

How to recognise a Fraud Predator

LEARNING FROM EXPERIENCE:

- ✓ Trust your instincts. If you think something is wrong, it most probably is wrong; Call a colleague to assist you in the conversation with the potential con-artist.
- ✓ Be aware of people who are well dressed and pushy, especially when dealing with financial transactions, i.e. looking for you to part with your or your employer's cash.
- ✓ If it seems too good to be true, then it is too good to be true.
- ✓ Don't let them play on your emotions. Cut the conversation short if you suspect something is wrong.
- ✓ Always report your suspicions to the authorities even if you don't have definitive proof. If a con artist is at work in your industry or community, it will assist Police in building a profile.

{7}

Terrorist Financing By Fraud

> *"Freedom itself was attacked this morning by a faceless coward, and freedom will be defended."*
> President George W Bush

We all remember what we were doing on the morning of September 11th 2001. A horrific time, that left many people dead, wounded or missing. So many years have passed since 9/11 yet we still live in the shadow of these evil acts. We have seen two wars in Iraq and Afghanistan, the successful hunt for Osama Bin Laden, multiple changes in laws and legislation including increased airline security procedures and the establishment of the Department of Homeland Security in North America. We remember, and must never forget, that terrorism is very much an ever- present threat to our society,

Universal Scams & Fraud Detection

liberties and all that we value and which we have come to take for granted, our liberty and freedom. As you read these words I would ask that you spare a thought for the brave American, British and other Coalition forces who continue to put their lives in harm's way so that we can continue to enjoy our freedom.

Before we take a closer look at terrorist financing we should first define the word terrorism. According to the Oxford English dictionary terrorism is defined as:

"The unlawful use or threatened use of force or violence by a person or an organized group against people or property with the intention of intimidating or coercing societies or governments, often for ideological or political reasons."

Acts of terrorism such as 9/11, the Bali bombings of 2002 and the London bombings in 2005, all required financing or hard cash for the terrorists to plan and carry out their evil deeds. All terrorists organisations, such as Al Qaeda, require finance in order to pursue their aims. This money is used to create bombs, recruit and train its members, travel costs and other expenses in order to plan for future terrorist attacks. It is important, and now an international legal requirement, for all banks and financial organisations to report suspect transactions to their respective governments. The identification of

Terrorist Financing By Fraud

suspect financial transactions also yields powerful intelligence to the security services such as MI6, or the CIA.

According to a report from the National Commission on Terrorist Attacks upon the United States of America, the total estimated cost of financing the 9/11 terrorist attack to Al Qaeda was between US$400,000 and US$500,000. There has been much research into the cost by both government and university academics. The 2005 London bombings are estimated at costing the terrorists US$15,600 (University of Maryland's National Consortium for the Study of Terrorism.) These costs are surprisingly low when you consider the damage caused to people's lives and the harm done to the global economy. It is imperative that the global community of financial organisations work with regulatory bodies and law enforcement to reduce the flow of funds to terrorist organisations.

There are key ways that terrorists obtain their funds, which includes the abuse of charity donations, crime such as fraud, state sponsored terrorism and from their members and organisations or individuals who sympathise with the idealism of the terrorist. It was well publicised that terrorist organisations in Northern Ireland received charity donations for "the cause" from North America. However, since 9/11 all such charity donations have ceased, including a reduction in state sponsored terrorism. This has made terrorists look for new opportunities

Universal Scams & Fraud Detection

to raise funds. Drug trafficking, Credit Card fraud and Counterfeiting of goods, including DVD's and Sports clothing, all well know items, have all proved to be a valuable source of funding.

According to the World Customs Organisation, the international trading of counterfeit goods has a value of US$600 billion a year which equates to approximately 6% of the world trade. It is difficult to estimate how much is going to fund terrorism. In 2004, US$1.2 million worth of vehicle brake pads were seized. Interpol's Secretary General, K Noble, stated that *"Linking the Hezbollah to counterfeit brake parts shows not only the link between terrorist financing and intellectual property crime, but also how intellectual property crime is not a victimless one – the potential danger to the public from this sort of criminal activity is too serious for governments and law enforcement to ignore."* But it's not just vehicle brake pads; Interpol advises that it's a full range of counterfeit products including pirated CD's and DVD's, designer clothes, computer software and cigarettes. Local country law enforcement agencies advise that there are links between counterfeit products and organised crime gangs who are also involved in other criminal activity. However, according to Interpol "intellectual property crime is becoming the preferred method of funding for a number of terrorist groups. There are enough examples now of the funding of terrorist groups in this way for us to worry about the threat to public safety. We must take preventative measures now."

Credit Card fraud which is covered in the banking chapter of this book is also a valuable tool for terrorists. The ability to make purchases by way of the identity theft of another's credit card makes it difficult for law enforcement to identify a potential terrorist. It is known that terrorists collate and harvest credit card data obtained for future use. In the UK, Tarig Al-Daour was in possession of 37,000 credit cards. In a report by Groupe d'action Financière it stated "it shows the vulnerability of credit cards to misuse for terrorist financing purposes and other illegal activities." Credit cards are also easier than carrying cash especially when travelling internationally. In addition, a credit card can be posted to an address from outside the jurisdition without raising suspicion.

Examples of Credit Cards & Terrorism
USA
Mr Nuradin Abdi, a Somalian national living in the United States, was convicted and eventually deported to Somalia, for providing stolen credit cards to an individual who was suspected of buying equipment for Al-Qaeda. It was reported that Mr Abdi allegedly collected the credit card numbers from his mobile phone (cell phone) business.

Universal Scams & Fraud Detection

Mr Abdi was allegedly involved with another member of Al-Qaeda and plotted to blow up a shopping centre in Columbus, Ohio. According to the US Department of Justice, Abdi admitted to FBI agents that he had provided material support to foreign terrorists. A Mr Iyman Faris, an associate of Abdi, was convicted of providing material support and conspiracy to provide material support to Al Qaeda and was sentenced to 20 years in jail.

UK

The Daily Mail reported that an Algerian man contributed to making £250,000 for terrorism from conspiracy to defraud banks and credit card companies. The individual advised that he had no knowledge that the money was being used to fund terrorism. In summing up, the Judge stated "Exactly how much you knew about the scale of the conspiracy it is impossible to know. What you certainly did know was that it was a sophisticated fraud involving the manufacture of false cards. You should understand that the Crown has not tried to say that you knew that the proceeds of those cards were used to fund terrorist organisations."

See second UK case covered in Chapter 13 – Banks, Credit Cards & Cybercrime

Australia

In Melbourne Australia, a Muslim cleric Abdul Benbrika, along with five others, plotted a terrorist attack to blow up

Terrorist Financing By Fraud

the Melbourne Cricket Ground. Had they been successful in their terrorist endeavours, an estimated 90,000 people could have been killed or injured at the Cricket Ground. As reported in the New York Times, it was stated that "During the court case, the prosecution claimed that Benbrika had told his followers that Osama bin Laden was a "great man" and that it was permissible to kill men, women and the aged". He said, "it would take at least 1,000 deaths to persuade the Australian government to withdraw from Iraq and Afghanistan."

It was also reported that one of the witnesses, a Mr Izzydeen Atik explained at the court case, how he purchased airplane tickets and mobile phones for the terrorist group using stolen credit cards.

The airline tickets purchased by Mr Atik were for the terrorist group using assumed or false identities. According to Interpol, only a handful of countries around the world screen air passengers against Interpol's database of stolen passports. In recent times it is hard to believe that two Iranians were able to board and fly on the missing Malaysian airliner. Some ten years after 9/11, ABC News reported that federal agents working undercover were still in a position to obtain American passports using false identities. An Irish case involving the convicted Texan, Jeremy Cochran, used the stolen identities of dead Irish

Universal Scams & Fraud Detection

babies to obtain numerous genuine Irish passports. This case brought to light another loop hole that needs to be tightened. There is now, more then ever, a need to introduce biometrics in passports, in the prevention of the theft of passports.

{8}

Interview Techniques

"We are a fact-gathering organization only. We don't clear anybody. We don't condemn anybody."

J. Edgar Hoover

The above statement identifies and explains the role of the investigator. It is their duty to gather the facts and evidence of the case and to present it to the client, the law enforcement agency or to the court. Interviewing witnesses and the recording of statements are key skills in the investigating process. Evidence should only be obtained by the fraud investigator in a fair and coherent way. Statements should only include factual evidence and not opinion. A statement from an individual accused of a criminal offence must be taken by the investigating police officer. Although this chapter is written for the benefit of a financial crimes investigator, it is possibly to adopt the guidelines for use in workplace incidents or Health & Safety investigations.

During my years of taking statements and interviewing witnesses and claimants, I have always used the PEACE model, which is an invaluable model for obtaining a credible statement. A statement from a credible witness is a crucial part of the investigation and evidence gathering process. Statements are considered "direct evidence" and if presented by way of evidence in court, needs to stand up to scrutiny.

- ✓ *P – Plan. Plan your interview and prepare specific questions*
- ✓ *E – Engage. Engage the person you are interviewing. Listen to them and take notes*
- ✓ *A – Ask. Ask questions and be specific*
- ✓ *C – Conclude the interview: be polite and professional at all times*
- ✓ *E – Explain and Evaluate. Explain the importance of the statement and evaluate any possible evidence within the statement.*

Plan

As with any task or conducting investigations, planning is critical. Before carrying out an interview, planning the interview structure, timing and the line of questions is paramount. A good investigator will examine all documentation,

Interview Techniques

evidence such as CCTV video footage, accident report forms and police or fire-officer reports before conducting the interview. Planning the important questions and building the main questions around some 'gentle' get to know you questions, will result in an effective interview.

The interview location should be chosen in advance. For example, it is not advisable to interview someone in their home, unless there are two investigators conducting the interview. This is to ensure the safety of the investigator. An ideal location, away from the home and the office, is a quiet hotel in which interviews can be held in a public and yet relaxing location. If carrying out an interview in an office environment, a private office away from other interested staff is required. The person being interviewed should be allowed sit closest to the exit and be free to leave the interview at any time.

Engagement:
It is most important to correctly engage with the interviewee, so think of it almost like a job interview. Reassuring the witness and making them feel relaxed will empower the investigator to gain greater respect from the witness, who in turn will deliver more accurate information. The investigator should engage the person with some general conversation, before settling down to take the formal statement. Always ask them to relate what they

know about the incident before putting their statement in writing. This should be relaxed and informal. Body language is also important - always sit back with nothing in your hands and relax as if talking to a friend about a football match. By engaging the person in some general conversation, it will hopefully make them feel relaxed which in turn may open them up to further disclosure of facts.

It is important that, before you commence writing the formal statement, you make the person aware of the reason for the interview. A person giving a formal statement to an investigator must be made aware that the statement has evidential value and that there may be a need, in the future, to attend court and give evidence based on the facts contained within the statement.

Ask:

The investigator should ask specific direct open ended questions, such as "tell me about yourself?" or "describe what you saw?" Asking these types of questions will enable the witness to deliver more valuable information instead of the less revealing yes / no answers. It will also permit the investigator to determine if the witness is cooperating and how they would stand up to being questioned in a court of law. The five W's should also be included in the main feature of the interview

Who?   What?   Where?   Why?   When?

Interview Techniques

The statement should include only factual information on what they have witnessed; the witness's opinions and/or feelings should not be included. The investigator should however take note of any subjective answers for future considerations.

Conclude:

On completion of the interview the investigator should take a few moments to consider the statement of fact as put forward by the witness and that all the necessary facts have been covered. The investigator should then read the statement back to the witness. In addition, the witness should be given a copy of the statement and invited to sign and date it. This would then be co-signed or witnessed by the investigator. I would advise that, if the witness has retained legal representation, the legal representative should be invited to review the statement before the witness signs. I would also recommend asking the person if they have any questions.

Explain & Evaluate:

On completion of the interview the witness should be advised of the next step in the process. It could simply be that the matter is now concluded or that it will be passed to a Manager or Solicitor for further consideration.

After the interview, the investigator should then evaluate the statement and cross-check with any notes taken during the interview. There is also a need to validate the statement of fact by either proving that the evidence provided in the statement is correct and factual or that it is false. This is done by "walking" (or reviewing) the statement, confirming the factual evidence within the statement as being true. For example the person may have stated that there were four people in a bank at the time of a robbery when CCTV proves there where only two people.

CONFESSIONS:

On vary rare occasions, the interviewee may provide a confession. If this happens, it is most important that you call a third party into the interview to witness the admission. This can be difficult if interviewing a person in a public location and this possibility should be considered at the planning stage of the interview.

I recall an interview at a house located in a remote area on the west coast of Ireland. The house had sustained severe damage from a fire and I was investigating the subsequent insurance claim. According to the insured, he was living in the house with his wife and young child. However, during the course of the interview (which took place at the house), post arrived addressed to a different person. When I showed the letters to the man and questioned him on the same, he confessed that the house was a rented property and that he had not been living

Interview Techniques

there. This was a fundamental principle of the insurance policy which was not disclosed at inception. As a result, the claim was declined. I ensured that a third party witnessed the confession and countersigned the statement.

On another occasion, an individual confessed, during an interview, to stealing mobile telephones from his employer. As the interview was being held at the employer's offices, I was in a position to call a manager to witness the confession and sign the statement. As mentioned, confessions are rare but if managed correctly can lead to an expeditious conclusion to an investigation.

LESSONS LEARNED:

- ✓ All evidence and documents should be reviewed before arranging an interview
- ✓ Set a location that is suitable and non-threatening to the interviewee
- ✓ Let the interviewee sit nearer to the door, so they feel they can exit at any time
- ✓ If possible, use a laptop and mobile printer as this will permit you to type the statement, make any changes and print during the interview
- ✓ Always give the witness a copy of the statement and make sure that every page is signed and dated by both the interviewee and yourself
- ✓ Adopt the PEACE model, when carrying out the interview
- ✓ Evaluate all evidence and consider the background of the witness, especially motives and connections
- ✓ Determine if it is possible to corroborate the statement with any other evidence?
- ✓ If you think you might obtain a confession, always call a third party into the interview as a witness

{9}

Surveillance

"Facebook is not your friend, it is a surveillance engine."
Richard Stallman

Surveillance is the observation or monitoring of the movements of an individual, who, in the investigation business, is known as the 'subject' or 'target.' The deployment of surveillance can be a costly exercise for organisations who engage the services of an untrained or licensed surveillance operative. However a planned surveillance operation by professional investigators can bring fruitful results, which can be used as evidence within a court of law. It is important to note that in most western countries surveillance is legal, as long as certain laws are not broken, such as trespass, civil rights and data protection. However in some middle-east countries surveillance of any description is illegal.

There are different types of surveillance, which includes foot surveillance, cars and motorcycle surveillance to aircraft and drone surveillance similar to that deployed by the United States Army in Iraq. In the main a civil investigator will be limited to foot and vehicle surveillance.

Consideration should also be given to covert surveillance, such as Closed Circuit Television (CCTV) as used in retail environments and airports, to covert body cameras and other electronic devices. I served as a trainee private investigator under the watchful eye of Sam Carroll, partner in Sleator Carroll investigations. I credit Sam with teaching me all I know about surveillance and the training I received has served me well. Surveillance is not something you can learn from a book; there is a need to learn surveillance from numerous hours of working with professionals in the field. The key requirements for a surveillance professional, is having the ability to blend into ones surroundings, patience and being open to any possibilities.

One of the key problems of a surveillance operation is you simply don't know what type of environment you will be operating in. Unless you are a member of a law enforcement

Surveillance

agency, you will have a limit on your manpower and budget. The surveillance or stakeout may commence in a standard housing estate and by the end of the surveillance, you may be on a construction site, airport or an office environment. The problem is the investigator must tail or follow the subject and you simply don't know where that will take you. Having suitable clothes or the ability to change them to suit your environment is important.

There is also a need to give consideration to the choice of vehicle used by the investigator. In real life, no private investigators will drive a red Ferrari on the job like Magnum pi. Most professional investigators operate in standard vehicles as nondescript as possible.

Thought needs to be given to photographic equipment for the recording of the subject's activities. When I commenced in the business, a standard 35mm camera with a 300mm lens was the equipment along with a notebook and pen. Nowadays standard equipment includes digital camcorders with micro SD memory, covert cameras, hidden within key rings or pens and a digital notebook for recording of dates and times of surveillance activity. Even the introduction of the mobile phone has made surveillance easier as communication between surveillance agents is of paramount importance.

Universal Scams & Fraud Detection

It is important to emphasise that law enforcement surveillance is completely different to civil investigating. The police or law enforcement agents are looking for evidence that will assist with criminal investigations, perhaps linking two known individuals or tailing a known criminal gang before they commit a crime, such as an armed robbery. A civilian or private investigator is generally looking for "contradictory" evidence. This may be used in the defence of an insurance claim, or to prove infidelity in a matrimonial investigation. Surveillance is also deployed in many other circumstances including tracing of witnesses, locating assets and monitoring of employee activity.

Undercover surveillance is generally only utilised in criminal investigations. However on occasion it is deployed in civil surveillance, but only when the circumstances deem it necessary. An example of this may be an individual who is claiming he is unable to work. The surveillance agent observes the target driving a taxi and hires the taxi recording the subject. This evidence would then be reviewed by a legal professional and consideration given for the provision of the evidence in court. Another example of undercover surveillance is placing an agent in the workplace as an employee. This is normally only utilised when there is a suspicion of staff theft.

Surveillance

Tips for Successful Surveillance:

- ✓ Carry out preliminary enquiries on your subject of investigation; establish as much intelligence as possible
- ✓ If possible have 2 x Agents and vehicles for the surveillance operation, with radio or phone contact
- ✓ Ensure all electronic equipment such as cameras, phones, radios and digital recorders are fully charged and working. Make sure you have a full tank of fuel in both vehicles
- ✓ If using tracking devices, ensure they are legal in your country of operation.
- ✓ Calls of Nature. Give consideration to toilet and eating needs. From experience as soon as you leave your observation point for a "call of nature", something happens
- ✓ Surveillance notes must not contain opinion. Only the facts of the surveillance should be recorded in your notebook and copied into the final report
- ✓ If you lose your subject, keep a note of travelled route and check the vicinity in an attempt to relocate the subject and the vehicle
- ✓ If utilising foot surveillance, try to blend into your surroundings and always keep the subject within your line of vision
- ✓ If ever questioned with the words "are you following me?" make an excuse and leave, never admit to surveillance of a subject, unless being questioned by a member of law enforcement

Universal Scams & Fraud Detection

COUNTER-SURVEILLANCE

The terminology of counter surveillance refers to the prevention and detection of surveillance against individuals or organisations. This may include sweeping or searching for electronic bugging devices, which are deployed for obtaining information and secrets, which is considered to be espionage within the corporate environment. I personally witnessed the United States Secret Service in operation during President Bill Clinton's first visit to Ireland in 1995. At this time I was employed by Pinkerton's and we provided a support service to the embassy. Obviously I cannot write about specifics, but in my view the US Secret Service provided an extraordinary level of expertise to the President and his family.

British Police and Police Service of Northern Ireland (PSNI) are also trained in identifying if they are the targets of surveillance activity. At this level having this training can be a matter of life and death to the officer.

Counter surveillance techniques are also deployed by criminals against law enforcement, from simply driving into a dead end, or walking into a shop and immediately exiting. These signs are not noticeable to the ordinary person, however a trained surveillance agent can spot these observations and deploy tactics such as changing surveillance vehicle or agent.

Surveillance

Of course if you are a law abiding citizen, but have reason to suspect you are under unwarranted surveillance then you should inform your local police as the surveillance could be of a criminal nature.

{10}

Retail Fraud & Theft

"I would not put a thief in my mouth to steal my brains."
William Shakespeare, Othello

The criminal justice Theft & Fraud Offences Laws, cover a vast array of financial institutions. However we should also give consideration to retail shops and outlets. Any retailer will inform you that they have to build a minimum of 10% into their retail price for "shrinkage" or unexplained losses in stock. This is, yet again, another example of just who pays for the retail crime, "you do" the customer who chooses to make a purchase from a shop.

According to the UK's centre for retail research, it is estimated that the Global cost of retail crime is US$119 billion and growing. The vast majority of the cost relates to shoplifters, 43%; Employee theft came a close second at 35%; internal errors, normally incorrect pricing, amounted to 16% and fraud and theft by suppliers and vendors amounted to 6%.

In North America, retail losses amounted to almost US$42 billion. In Europe it was US$48 billion, the UK, US$7.8 billion and Ireland US$600 million. The Irish police, An Garda Siochana, deployed a successful strategy for combating shoplifting, involving uniformed and plain clothes Detectives. The Gardai estimate that retail theft in Ireland would be equal to an annual tax of €348.91 on every household in the country.

These losses all contributed to a reduction in the retailers' balance sheet and had a significant impact on employment opportunities for many individuals.

I commenced my career as a Retail Security Officer and Store Detective at the youthful age of eighteen. It was an excellent foundation for obtaining an introduction to fraud, investigation and crime prevention. Dealing with retail crime, is also very much at the coalface of criminality. It was also one of my first experiences of 'foot surveillance', following suspects on foot. Retail outlets employ various forms of Security, including Store Security Officers and plain clothes detectives, electronic tagging of products, CCTV video recording and warning signs such as "thieves will be prosecuted." Whilst all of these are effective in their own right, in my view the best way of preventing theft in a retail environment is by employing, training and managing well motivated staff.

A simple way of identifying a potential thief or 'shop lifter' is to simply approach them and ask *"May I help You?"* This open-ended question will either identify a potential opportunistic thief or a normal customer who is looking to make a purchase. Observing the behaviour and body language of the customer, makes it easy to determine any potential risk. The staff being open, friendly and professional will minimise the chance of any false arrest claims resulting in litigation. Under no circumstances should a uniformed Security Officer make contact with members of the public unless first approached. We live in an all too litigious society; "false arrest" claims can be difficult to defend and costly.

Again we need to consider just who exactly pays for theft from shops. Well once again the answer is simply, *You do*. The cost of stolen stock needs to be covered by the retail price paid by you, the customer. Personally, I don't mind paying a few percent in my purchases to cover the cost of theft prevention, but I do have a problem in covering the cost of already stolen items.

Universal Scams & Fraud Detection

Like all other forms of theft and fraud, there are many reasons why individuals choose to steal from shops. However it has been proven that there is a direct link between drug usage and shoplifting. We also have to face the reality that it is difficult to prevent retail theft from busy shops and department stores.

Many of the shop-lifters or thieves who steal from shops are well known to the retail security and general staff. Some of the more professional con artists will use disguises, including false wigs and other disguises to gain access to the stores. The following are some examples of professional scams occurring in a retail environment:

DRESSING ROOM SCAM:

A well known professional con-artist used to try on clothes in the dressing room then wear the clothes underneath her clothes when exiting the shop. This problem is easily resolved by having a staff member issue a tag displaying the number of items taken into the dressing room. This tag along with the garments is then returned to the staff member on leaving the dressing room or handed in at the check-out desk when paying for the goods. The local store which did not have this system in place estimated that they lost circa €15,000 (US$20,000) in stock from the individual in the dressing room scam.

Retail Fraud & Theft

THE STEALING TEAM:

This well established scam involves two or more thieves who work the store together. The scam generally involves a small shop which specialises in selling high-value ladies clothing. Three professional perpetrators or thieves would enter the store on a relatively quiet day, most likely early on a Monday or Tuesday morning, when the store would have minimal staff on duty. The first thief would engage the staff member, perhaps asking them about a potential purchase. The second perpetrator would select an item and then quickly pass it to the third perpetrator who would immediately exit the store. Even if the staff member observed the second person stealing the item and stopped them, they would no longer have it in their possession. The way the law is structured, this scenario would potentially leave the staff member open to ligation for making a false allegation or false arrest.

THE TECHNICAL SCAM:

An individual who operated in North America was a bit of a genius when it came to computers, in particular bar codes. The individual specialised in stealing valuable toys from shops, which he even 'paid for' at the check-outs.

His scam involved the manipulation of the electronic bar coding on the price tags, to a lower price than was originally placed on the item by the retailer. He would reduce the price of

Universal Scams & Fraud Detection

a high value toy from, say, US$100 to $20. The cashier would have no reason to suspect the customer and would accept the lower payment. The individual would then advertise and sell the item on internet websites such as EBay, as unwanted, unopened gifts at a knockdown prices of US$75. This financially lucrative scam cost retailers more than US$500,000 before the individual was apprehended.

DUTY FREE SHOPLIFTING:

It is well known within the security industry that, with the onset of cheap airline travel, professional shoplifters are booking flights and stealing while in the airports duty free areas. High street retail outlets employ certain measures of security which, as effective as they are, generate difficulties for the thieves in plying their trade. However in secure zones such as airside in airports, retailers have been letting their guard down.

One such example involved a Polish couple who regularly flew between Poland and Bristol, Glasgow and Edinburgh. The two specialised in robbing high value perfume. The couple made the trips on numerous occasions before being spotted on CCTV placing (unpaid for) perfume in their carry bags. When stopped by Airport Police, they had in their possession 40 boxes of perfume worth £2,635. Both pleaded guilty and have since been deported from the UK.

Retail Fraud & Theft

LESSONS LEARNED:

- ✓ Expensive items to be displayed as far as possible from the exit
- ✓ 'Thieves will be prosecuted' signs to be displayed
- ✓ Use an electronic security tagging system on expensive items
- ✓ Train all staff in security awareness
- ✓ Be aware of individuals who are more interested in looking at the staff than items for purchase, especially if wearing bulky clothing and carrying bags
- ✓ Contract a Security Officer or Store Detective for busy periods
- ✓ Have the pay desk as close to the exit as possible, so that the potential thief will have to walk past the pay desk in order to exit the store. Obviously keep minimal cash at the pay desk
- ✓ Try and keep the store as tidy as possible and keep the floor space viewable with minimal corners
- ✓ Always issue a receipt for all purchases no matter how small the economic value of the purchased item
- ✓ Use CCTV for covering cash tills and blind spots within the store

Universal Scams & Fraud Detection

- ✓ Recognition of Presence - Be friendly open and polite.
- ✓ Greet your customers openly welcome them to your store and also make sure to say "goodbye."

Say "Hello" to the potential shoplifter; Let them know that they are not invisible to your staff.

{11}

Employee Theft:

"The employer generally gets the employees he deserves."

J. Paul Getty

It should be noted, from the outset, that the majority of staff are honest and trustworthy and would never consider stealing from their employer. However, there are opportunistic and premeditated unscrupulous individuals who would have no hesitation in stealing. This stealing might be a case of simply removing stock for themselves or selling onwards, stealing cash or something more complex, such as fraud. Although cash is desired by the thief, we should also give consideration to "time", such as falsifying time-sheets and also unauthorised use of equipment, such as company cars, computers or other activities.

Universal Scams & Fraud Detection

According to the United States Chamber of Commerce, employee theft is estimated at costing circa US$30 billion a year. The report also advises that on average 75% of employee thefts go undetected.

There is also a need to consider employee espionage and selling of company confidential information to competitors. This can be difficult to detect and even harder to prosecute. The best method of prevention is by conducting audits and developing protocol working documents. These documents should be considered "live documents" which are reviewed and updated regularly.

Before an employer offers a position to an individual, it is crucial to carry out an elaborate interview, together with a full background verification. The background verification is an important part of the recruitment process and should be carried out by a skilled individual.

It is also important to watch for "unexplained" gaps in employment history and to always check the authenticity and accuracy of any references. It is far easier to prevent the employment of a dishonest individual then it is to detect and remove the employee from the business at a later date.

Employee Theft:

Preventing Employee Theft

- ✓ Build a Strong working relationship with your staff, create friendships while maintaining professionalism
- ✓ Implement a Code of Ethical Behaviour, including warnings of termination, within contracts of employment
- ✓ Keep negativity out of the workforce. Respect your staff and they will work well for you
- ✓ Engage the services of a professional security company and install CCTV
- ✓ Access control and restricted access to high risk areas
- ✓ Develop protocols and procedures
- ✓ Monitor the removal of rubbish from the business. (A favourite for internal thieves when stealing company stock)
- ✓ Audit workflow and systems and implement a strategy to mitigate any loss opportunities
- ✓ Set up a confidential, anonymous, way for your employees to tip off management of suspicions
- ✓ If there is a report or incident of employee theft, always investigate and if needed call on your security provider to assist with the investigation

Examples of Employee Scams:

The Over Trusting Employer

I recall a case on which I worked whilst I was a trainee Private investigator. The client owned and operated a small public house and hotel. He was an elderly gentleman who trusted his staff as he had 'no reason not to trust them.' They had been employed by him for years. The owner would work in the bar each morning, but would be gone by midday and would not return until the following day. However he had no explanation as to why the turnover from the bar business was lower on weekend nights, when this should have been the busiest period of the week.

On the advice of his accountant, the owner approached my then employer and we arranged a test purchase or "mystery shopper" in the bar. A test purchase is effectively an undercover private investigator acting as a customer and observing the actions of the staff member during a transaction.

According to the client, he employed four full time barman and two junior bar boys who worked on a part time basis.

While sitting at the busy bar, we observed a senior and a junior barman working. On making our purchases, we received receipts and change, with nothing appearing out of the ordinary. This test purchasing was repeated over the next two weekends with similar outcomes. On meeting with the client, we were dismayed and confused as, although we had our suspicions, we could not explain why the cash take was down. On

Employee Theft:

all occasions, we observed the barman putting the money in the cash register and issuing a receipt to the customer.

We agreed to carry out a further two weekends of test purchasing. The client remained stubbornly firm, that the reasons for the losses were not down to dishonest actions by his staff. On the next periods of test purchasing we marked the money which we would use for the transaction with a special pen which is only visible under an ultraviolent light. We also noted the serial numbers of the currency notes. Once again we sat at the bar and observed the barman and a junior serving several customers, issuing change and receipts from the cash register. Once again all appeared normal.

A further meeting was arranged with the client and yet once again we explained that we could find no evidence to explaining his reduction in the cash take. The bar was busy with customers making purchases. The cash take was again down. The money we had marked with the ultra violet pen was missing. Yet again, the client was adamant his staff would not steal from him, but there was no other explanation. It was a complete mystery.

It was then that a simple comment from the senior Private Investigator effectively solved the case!

Universal Scams & Fraud Detection

"One thing that is strange is that they use the cash register beside the phone at a ratio of 3:1 as against the larger cash register underneath the whiskey bottles. Sometimes they even walk past the large cash register to use the smaller one"

The owner of the bar, went pale in his complexion, glared at his accountant and put his head in his hands. There was an uneasy silence for a few moments. The senior investigator looked somewhat dismayed with the accountant also looking somewhat shocked.

The client then stated

"I only have one cash register!"

After further investigation it was established that each of the four senior barmen had purchased their own cash register. Initially, they only used it a couple of times a night but then greed set it and eventually, they were using it at an approximate ratio of 3:1. All four confessed to their crimes and resigned from their employment.

I later heard that the owner of the bar was so hurt and upset at the actions of his "loyal staff" that he sold the pub. The accountant estimated that, the loss sustained was in excess of €120,000.

Employee Theft:

THE GREEDY CAR PARK ATTENDANT

Another example of staff fraud in a retail environment was a car park attendant responsible for the taking of cash as cars entered a car park facility.

The car park, operated an all-day rate, had spaces for sixty two cars with a charge rate of €7.50 per day and was nearly always full. Based on an average fill rate of 90% per day, this would have given a daily turnover of circa €418.50 per day or €2,092.50 per week, based on five days of operation.

The car park attendant's duty was to simply lift a barrier when a car entered; issue a ticket and collected the money. The exit barrier automatically lifted when customers approached the barrier. In an effort to prevent theft by staff, the exit barrier clicked off an electronic counter, recording the number of times the barrier opened. There was only one employee who worked 60 hours per week. Suspicion was raised when the car park attendant had to take two weeks off as he needed an operation. In the period of his absence, the turnover was between €400 and €420 per day, whereas, when the employee in question was at the car park, the turnover was circa €350 - €375 per day, or circa €40 less per day.

An investigation including early morning surveillance, determined that the car park entrance barrier was being left open in

Universal Scams & Fraud Detection

the morning at the busy period permitting "regular" customers to enter the car park, without a ticket being issued. The attendant would simply take cash, at what was believed to be a "reduced rate" of circa €5 per day from the regular customer.

The individual confessed to the scam and was dismissed without criminal prosecution. It was estimated that the daily scam had been operating for two years at approximately €200 per week, a loss of circa €20,000 over the two year period. A simple scam which was topping up the employee's wages with a nice tidy tax-free amount.

The Ghost Employee

One of the highest costs to any business is 'staff payroll'. The management of the payroll system is crucial to the overall financial success of the business. Budgets and protection of staff costs must be established at the beginning of the year and then monitored and maintained.

A Security Guarding company operated with 82 staff, providing security officers to mainly industrial and retail outlets. The payroll was handled by a young female member of staff. One of the security officers had a heart attack and was off work for a six month period. As it was a small company, he did not receive any payment whilst off work. However the young

Employee Theft:

pay-roll lady diverted his weekly pay to a new bank account which was of course in her name. By the time she was caught by Police, she had received almost US$12,000. In place of receiving a jail sentence she agreed to pay back the money to her former employer.

THE LAPTOP SCAM:

Markets are popular places for people to make purchases at reduced prices. Once again, when making any such purchases you should trust your intuition. If it is too good to be true, then it isn't true. Some markets sell genuine products which have been passed to the market to sell as it is being replaced by new stock or a new model. However many items are not genuine and are counterfeit products.

One scam, which affected a well-respected business man, involved the purchase of a new Laptop from a market stall at a reduced price of €250, the full retail price was €799. This was an excellent deal or so the man assumed. He was permitted to examine the laptop in great detail before making the purchase, which came in an authentic box. After much deliberating, the business man decided to make the purchase for his son and haggled with the salesman to an agreed knock-down price of €225. He was handed the laptop box and was delighted with his purchase.

Universal Scams & Fraud Detection

When the business man got home, he handed the Laptop box to his son who was delighted with his new gift. However when the son opened the box, all it contained was a copy of a phone book. The business man, as well as another three individuals, had made similar purchases of a laptop at the 'reduced' or 'knock down' price. Complaints were made to the Police but the salesman was never tracked down leaving four angry conned customers.

As previously advised, now more then ever with the financial recession, there is a need to ensure staff are not helping themselves to the profits or stealing items for personal use or selling onwards.

Employee Theft:

> **LEARNING FROM EXPERIENCE**
> - ✓ Be aware of staff who don't take annual leave / holidays, are they really that committed to your company / business?
> - ✓ Staff who are living beyond their earnings, flash cars, jewellery etc. Don't accept that the item belongs to the husband or wife of the employee. Ask questions, and conduct background investigations
> - ✓ An employee who answers your queries with questions or threats of legal action, should raise concern
> - ✓ CV details not complete – Carry out a full background check on all staff or contract out to a specialist. Spending money on staff vetting before employment will save you money in the long term. Prevention is much more cost effective then detection
> - ✓ It is the duty of the employer or manager to police staff
> - ✓ Provide training for all your staff on fraud awareness and theft prevention
> - ✓ If you have the evidence of fraud or theft, report to the Police and always prosecute
>
>

{12}

Identity Theft

> "People need to be more aware and educated about identity theft. You need to be a little bit wiser, a little bit smarter and there's nothing wrong with being sceptical. We live in a time when if you make it easy for someone to steal from you, someone will."
>
> Frank Abagnale

The most valuable possessions you have are your identity and your character. The idea of someone stealing your identity is terrifying. Unfortunately it is a growing problem. According to the Federal Bureau of Investigation, identity theft is currently the fastest growing crime in North America. There are two types of identity theft; the first is theft of the identity of a credit card or bank account, the second, and far more serious, is a person's national identity. This is taking not only the individuals identity but also the passport of the nation of which that person is a citizen.

If we look at the history of identity theft, we can go as far back as the first book of the bible, Genesis. It is written that Jacob, in order to get his father's blessing for being the first born son, covered himself with goat skin. His father, who had poor eyesight, gave the blessing to Jacob thinking that it was his other son, Esau. And so the first identity theft deception was played out and the financial gain of the father's land and possessions were given to Jacob.

To an untrained investigator or non-law enforcement person, identity theft may appear complex but in reality, as with the above example, identity theft is generally easy to perpetrate against an unsuspecting individual.

We can take a look at the infamous outlaws of 1880's America and most notably the criminal exploits of Butch Cassidy and The Sundance Kid made famous by Hollywood. These individuals would rob the railroad and banks and then simply disappear without trace. They were known to have multiple identities which made the tracking and investigation difficult for the then law enforcement and the Pinkerton Detectives. Using 'Wanted' posters and networking with Sheriffs made it possible for the Pinkerton Agents to track these outlaws.

Identity Theft

Today, there is a clear and present danger of terrorist activity against many nations. According to the FBI website *"A stolen identity is a powerful cloak of anonymity for criminals and terrorists…and a danger to national security and private citizens alike."* I find these words terrifying, especially considering the terrorist attacks of recent times.

All nations who enjoy liberty, justice and freedom have a need to protect the identity of their citizens. The identity theft of an individual's passport is a serious matter, not just for the individual, but also for the nation. It was widely reported that, in 2010, the FBI infiltrated a Russian spy ring in New York. Ten alleged Russian spy agents were deported from America. It was reported that six of the Russian spy's were travelling on forged Irish passports, belonging to Irish citizens who had previously visited Russia.

In 2010 agents from the Israeli Secret Service, Mossad, allegedly carried out the assassination of Hamas leader Mahmoud-al-Mabhouh in a hotel in Dubai. These assassins were also thought to be travelling on Irish Passports. In addition, the Irish Government expelled an official from the Israeli embassy based in Dublin for using forged Irish passports. Irish opposition TD Billy Timmons called on the government to question the Russian and Israeli governments on the use of the Irish passports. All of these political rumblings are very nice for political gain, however how would Ireland or any nation feel if terrorists used a citizens national identity for horrific terrorist atrocities such as 9/11.

It was also reported that 33,000 Irish passports were reported lost or stolen. These thefts of Irish passports also put honest Irish citizens under suspicion. The passport is supposed to be the most definitive and therefore most valuable document you have for proving your identity, especially when in a foreign country. In financial institutions such as banks, the passport is always the most sought after documentation in order to satisfy the requirements of anti-money-laundering and anti-terrorist-financing legislation. When a customer presents a passport as a proof of identity, it is generally accepted to be an official document issued by the country of citizenship.

The question has been asked why Irish passports are the choice of these governments secret security organisations. The answer is rather simple and, in the main, is a compliment to modern day Ireland. Irish citizens are popular in most countries around the world. Ireland has excellent relations with the United States of America, we speak English and we are a gateway to Europe. An Irish Passport is also a European Union passport granting permission to enter and stay in any European member countries.

Identity Theft

There is a clear need for the Irish government and all governments to take passport identity theft seriously. There is also a greater need to make the passport more secure, perhaps introducing biometric identification requirements, such as fingerprinting. Those of us who travel to the Unites States, are familiar with the security requirements for entering the United States as a tourist, enforced by the Department of Homeland Security. This process to gain entry includes prior, via the internet, luggage identification by photograph and fingerprinting. The United States is a target for many terrorist organisations, there is a clear need to profile all visitors in an effort to protect its citizens and visitors alike.

There are still questions unanswered about the disappearance of Malaysian Airlines flight MH370. The Boeing 777 was on a routine flight from Kuala Lumpur to Beijing and simply vanished. At the time of writing this book, the plane has not been found. It was reported that two Iranian passengers were travelling on false passports, belonging to two European citizens, an Austrian and an Italian. It is hard to believe and completely unacceptable that with the advancement in technology, any individual could travel on an international flight using a false or stolen passport.

In 2008, I was asked by my manager to write a training paper on identity theft. I had little or no experience of the topic at that time and was pleased when my manager received a promotion and forgot about the request. However in 2009, I was asked to investigate a suspect insurance claim involving Jeremy Cochran, a man from Dallas Texas, who was allegedly involved in a road traffic accident in County Kildare, about twenty miles west of Dublin. Little did I know how much knowledge and experience I was going to gain from this one particular case.

The man claimed he had sustained a back injury while he was walking in a remote park area, popular with dog walkers and joggers. The insured, a Polish national, whom the claimant advised he did not know, knocked him down causing severe back injury. After six weeks investigating, I had traced Cochran to Las Vegas and was able to obtain a Marriage certificate. This certificate was direct contradictory evidence, proving that he was married to the sister of the insured Polish man. This was enough to effectively throw out the claim and to make a considerable financial saving. However this was only the tip of the iceberg.

During the course of my investigation I came upon another name, which was a false identity used by the Texan. This second identity was stolen from a man living in Northern Ireland. When I cross checked this name with Insurance Link, it found a claim against another Irish insurance company. Risk

Identity Theft

Intelligence - Insurance Link, the Irish insurance industry fraud prevention system allows insurance companies to check identities against other insurer's claimants for claims history and verifications. This is a similar IT solution to ISO in North America.

The other insurance company provided me with an address in Dundalk, near the border with Northern Ireland. It also gave the name of their insured who was the Polish lady named on the marriage certificate. Unfortunately, this claim had been settled with a substantial payment being awarded to the man under the false identity. Amongst the insurance fraud community this is effectively known as a *'staged accident.'*

With the assistance of the Irish Garda Bureau of Fraud Investigation (GBFI) we discovered that Jeremy Cochran had opened an account in an Irish bank whilst using an official Irish passport as proof of his identity. This false passport permitted him to beat anti money-laundering legislation and to lodge the cheque received for the insurance claim, using the same false identity.

Another name also came to light during the investigation. Once again using the Risk Intelligence tool I was able to trace another claim payment by a different insurance company. An

Universal Scams & Fraud Detection

Irish passport was used as identity and a substantial payment was made by the insurance company. On this occasion the identity was that of an Irish baby who died just after his birth in 1975.

Over the course of the investigation, I established that five genuine Irish passports were issued to Cochran. Four of the identities belonged to deceased Irish babies. Harvesting these identities gave Cochran the ability to masquerade in the identities of Irish babies who had died at the time of their births circa 1975/76. Eventually Cochran was arrested in Dublin airport trying to board an international flight whilst travelling on an official Irish passport issued in the name of yet another baby who had died in 1975.

This mammoth investigation, which involved multiple jurisdictions would not have been possible without the assistance of the GBFI, US Secret Service, District Attorneys Office in Durant Oklahoma, the Sheriffs' departments in Dallas and Las Vegas, Colorado State Police, British Police and Polish investigators. In March 2011, he pleaded guilty to several counts of fraud and was sentenced to four years in jail. He has since been deported back to the Unites States of America.

Special recognition also to Ms Ron Smith Murphy of A Little Lifetime foundation who provided advice and support to the

Identity Theft

GBFI officers and to the parents of the children whose identity had been stolen.

The case made headline news in Ireland

In my 25 years of working in the security and financial investigation business, I have not come across a more professional and complex fraud. This case although covered under identity theft in this book, included so many other types of fraud and criminal activity, including insurance fraud. The most harrowing and personally upsetting of Cochran's crimes was the theft of the identities of innocent Irish babies who had died around the time of their birth. Following the publicity surrounding my book *"Someone Has Taken my Place"* which is based on the pursuit and apprehension of Jeremy Cochran, the mothers of two children whose identities were stolen, came forward and contacted me.. Mrs Fran Gibney and Mrs Ann Conroy. As a father of a deceased child, my son Andrew died at the time of his birth in 2003, I could relate to the pain and suffering of the parents.

Universal Scams & Fraud Detection

When a parent looses a baby at birth, or is told that the baby will die, there is nothing more harrowing or painful. Each situation is different, the baby like my son Andrew, may have died in the womb, or perhaps will live for a few seconds, minutes, maybe a day or even a week. The short time you have with your baby, builds into a precious memory and a bond that you will take with you for the remainder of your life. To have the babies identity stolen, some thirty five years later is summed up in the quote by Ryan Tubridy of RTE's *The Late Late Show* "It is like kicking the headstone of the baby."

A country like Ireland, or any country, has a duty to protect the identities of its citizens. This must not happen again but sadly I have no doubt that the identity theft of the deceased will continue to be a significant problem for the future.

The Late Late Show Television interview with the author and Anne Conroy is available for viewing on the author's website www.davidsnowauthor.com

Identity Theft

LEARNING FROM EXPERIENCE:

- ✓ Always do your best to protect your identity, never give out your personal details to anyone you don't know
- ✓ Shred any unneeded confidential documents, such as Credit Card statements, bank statements, and household utility bills. Remember in order to obtain a bank account you need a form of photographic identity such as a passport or driving license and two household utility bills, such as phone or electricity bills. Utility bills are valuable documents in the hands of an identity thief
- ✓ Obtain a credit report once a year. Check your credit rating and look for suspicious activity such as banks you *don't* use checking your credit rating
- ✓ By wary of any post you receive which is unsolicited. Don't ignore the post, make contact with the sender and query how they obtained your contact name and address
- ✓ If you move from your current address, let the post office know that you have moved to a new address

Universal Scams & Fraud Detection

There are 3 x basic steps which can protect your identity; which is covered under the word scam:

- ✓ S – Scarce: Be scarce with the personal information you issue
- ✓ C- Check: Check your credit report and status at least once a year
- ✓ A – Aware: Be aware of the potential of having your identity stolen
- ✓ M –Maintain: Maintain a record of all your invoices, utility bills and credit card statements

If you feel you've been the victim of identity theft, report it to your local law enforcement, such as the FBI as soon as possible. Ensure to ask for the record number (Pulse crime number in Ireland) and keep a record of all your dealings with law enforcement. You should also inform your bank, credit card company, insurance company and household utility providers of any potential identity theft.

{13}

Insurance Fraud

"The Crime you pay for"
International Association of Special Investigation Units
www.iasiu.org

The word "insurance" automatically conjures up images of boring men in boring grey coats discussing boring issues. But insurance fraud is most interesting as it affects each and every one of us who holds an insurance policy. Insurance Fraud also covers many interesting investigation opportunities, such as Arson, Forensics, Business Interruption, personal injury and robbery.

Insurance companies are commercial businesses and are obliged to make profits for their owners and shareholders. The

Universal Scams & Fraud Detection

cost of fraud has to be added to each premium and, according to the Insurance Fraud Bureau in the UK, insurance fraud is estimated at adding £45 sterling to the cost of every individual annual insurance premium.

In the United States, the FBI, advise insurance fraud is estimated at costing US$30 Billion. In Ireland, Insurance fraud is costing €200 million per annum, South Africa R4 billion and Australia $4 billion. Insurance fraud also generates job losses and causes other financial concerns for business owners. The cost of Public Liability and Employers Liability (Workers compensation in the USA) is one cost which has to be paid in advance of making a single cent from turnover.

I have been working within the insurance industry for over ten years. I find general insurance an incredibly boring subject which I would not have any interest in studying. However the International Association of Special Investigations Units (IASIU) is a professional global association which runs training events throughout the United States and Europe. The training is excellent and passing of the CIFI examination awards you with the Certified Insurance Fraud Investigator designation, which is well respected in North America and growing in Europe. This certification, which is insurance fraud specific, is of value to insurance investigators and a

Insurance Fraud

globally recognised skill set. I completed my CIFI examination at the IASIU conference in Germany in 2012. That said, the best knowledge and experience can only be gained from working in the field – from the fraudsters themselves.

Every year we see new attempts to defraud insurance companies. The best advice I can give any investigator is to simply keep an open mind to all possibilities.

Combating insurance fraud is difficult and immensely challenging. It can be broken into two specific areas which are fraud by the insured person or company, such as the fraudulent reporting of the theft of a car or other valuable item. The second is third party claims fraud which are insurance claims made by another individual against the insurance policy holder.

Although fraud investigators and Manager's work within the insurance arena, their work is completely different to that of a normal insurance executive. Insurance Fraud investigators do not, and should not, give advice to customers on polices or products. The Fraud investigators role largely exists in the prevention and detection of insurance fraud whilst staying as impartial as possible. Having an expert knowledge of the terms and conditions of insurance policies may be turned against the investigator in a court of law.

Universal Scams & Fraud Detection

The members of an anti-fraud team will use specially designed red flags or suspect signs, particular to each line of business. These systems are designed for the identification of suspect claims. These claims are then passed to the Special Investigation Unit (SIU) for a full investigation. The fraud investigator must prove that the insurance claim is either correct as stated by the claimant or not. It is an advantage and, in fairness to the claimant, if the fraud investigator is not versed or educated in the terms of the specific policy of insurance. The investigator is obliged to obtain all information of evidential value with regards to the statement of claim. That information is then passed to a claims operative or Manager. On the fraud investigator's advice, the Claims Manager determines if the claim should be settled in accordance with the terms of the policy or declined. If the claim is declined, the insured still has the option of taking legal advice or seeking an independent assessment from the financial services ombudsman.

Thanks to the efforts of organisations such as IASIU, Insurance Fraud is now recognised as a global scourge which affects all citizens. Insurance companies have retained fraud investigation personnel and are educating the public on the problem of fraud. However, the individual insurance companies can only do so much to protect themselves. Working together, collating and mining claims data from all insurance companies is the greatest deterrent to the occurrence

Insurance Fraud

of fraud. An example of this is the activity of the National Insurance Crime Bureau (NICB) in North America. Claims data from all insurance companies in the United States is filtered through an IT system, with suspect claims being investigated. Link analysis tools permits investigators to detect commonalities and links between different claims. There is a need to develop such a system in Europe in an effort to combat trans-national insurance fraud.

The general public can also assist in the combating of insurance fraud by reporting suspect claims to the insurance companies 'cheat' phone lines or to local law enforcement. Insurance companies all over the globe are now combating fraud for the benefit of all customers.

At the outset of this chapter I advised that insurance fraud is interesting because of the variety of scams we investigate. In general insurance, there are fraudulent claims in the following areas:
- Property
- Motor damage
- Motor Theft
- Motor Injury fraud
- Employers & Public Liability Fraud
- False theft of Jewellery and Art claims
- Travel insurance fraud

Universal Scams & Fraud Detection

All of the above can be complex and difficult to investigate. However, a well trained and experienced investigator can apply their knowledge to almost any investigation in any area of insurance. The following are cases which have been investigated by Insurance Fraud Investigators.

PROPERTY FRAUD - ARSON

Investigating fires can be difficult and requires the assistance of experts of forensic fire investigation. These specialists are for the most part, self-employed and provide their professional services to insurance companies and their appointed Loss Adjusters. One of the most important aspects of suspect property fire investigation is to have the forensic investigator at the scene of the fire as early as possible, ideally while the Police are still carrying out their scene of crime investigation. The reason for this is evidence will be lost with time. Most Forensic investigators also work with the Police and share knowledge, which is of mutual benefit.

One individual reported that, while he was away for an evening with his family, his house was destroyed by fire. The insurance fraud investigator was called in to investigate, as the policy of insurance had been issued only a short time previously. In his statement the claimant advised that he had left the house with his family and then received a telephone call, at about 11pm that evening, from a neighbour, telling him that

Insurance Fraud

his house was on fire. On the surface all appeared plausible and genuine. However, the insurance fraud investigator was suspicious of the story and did not like the burn patterns in the house. He decided to call in a fire forensic investigator.

The investigation was completed by the forensic fire investigator, revealing that the insurance investigator had been right to be suspicious. Typically, in an accidental fire, flames and smoke rise, but on this occasion, the flames and smoke were going downwards at one of the seats of fire.

There was also three seats of fire, or three locations in which the fire started. In a genuine fire, unless arson, there is normally only one seat of fire. The forensic investigator concluded that a plastic bath tub in the main upstairs bathroom had been filled with a flammable liquid and a small candle placed in the liquid. When the candle burnt down it permitted the candle flame to come into contact with the flammable liquid causing a fireball and significant damage. However, after a short period the bath melted which fell through the floor into the downstairs room. There was also no sign of forced entry into the house and this evidence was enough to dismiss the claim.

MOTOR DAMAGE FRAUD:

Motor damage accounts for a large proportion of claims for any insurance company. Having a skilled team is crucial for the success of any motor insurance fraud prevention strategy. It is also linked with motor personal injury, which requires medical experts to assist with the investigation. In addition to the internal claims staff, it is also important to have a skilled team of Motor Assessors to investigate damaged vehicles.

In one particular case, a motor assessor was not satisfied that the damage to a vehicle was recent. The damaged area of the vehicle was already rusting, which indicated that the damage was older than had been reported by the insured. An insurance investigator interviewed the insured who advised that he had driven the vehicle over some wet leaves lost control of the vehicle and crashed into a wall. The investigator inspected the wall which was clearly damaged. However, the investigator called to houses in the vicinity of the accident location. One of the residents recalled seeing a man, fitting the description of the insured, knocking down the wall with a lump hammer the previous evening.

The insurance investigator also checked the vehicle with Risk Intelligence Insurance Link and discovered that, not only had the vehicle been imported from the UK, but that it had been involved in an accident in the UK. The Motor Industry Anti-Fraud Theft Register UK (MIFTR) revealed that the vehicle had been the subject of an insurance claim the previous year. The investigator contacted a colleague in the UK who provided

Insurance Fraud

photographs of the damage to the vehicle. As expected, the damage was exactly the same. The insurance investigator put the evidence to the claimant. The claim was withdrawn in full and the matter was passed to the Police.

Motor Theft Fraud:

In Ireland, there are approximately 8,000 cars reported stolen each year, approximately 370,000 in the UK and 721,053 in the USA. (All figures have been acquired from confidential sources employed within vehicle law enforcement.) To deal with this, motor insurance companies must have a strong team of skilled and experienced investigators. There are also procedures in place with the police, such as, when a car is stolen, details are placed on a vehicle plate and chassis register of stolen vehicles. If somebody tries to register the ownership of the vehicle, then the Police and Insurance Company respond and take possession of the stolen vehicle.

One scam involved the reporting of the theft of a high value Mercedes to an insurance company. All appeared normal and the insurance company paid out €22,000 in compensation to the owner. However all was not what it seemed when the car was registered to a new owner.

On this occasion an innocent man had purchased the vehicle for a reduced price of €18,000. This was an excellent price for the Mercedes car and was 'too good to be true.' The unfortunate purchaser of the car had been scammed. The vehicle was seized by the Police and eventually returned to the insurance company who sold the vehicle at auction for €12,000, leaving a shortfall of €10,000. As the individual had effectively purchased a stolen vehicle, his €18,000 was gone. However all was not lost as the description provided by the purchaser was similar to the insured. The Police arrested the insured who confessed and was convicted in Court of fraud or deception against the insurance company. He was ordered to pay back the insurance company the difference of the €10,000 and also the €18,000 which he had obtained from the unfortunate man who purchased the car.

This was an excellent result for the insurance company. Unfortunately it was not the end of the matter. The following chart illustrates the complexity of insurance fraud and what happened next in the case.

Insurance Fraud

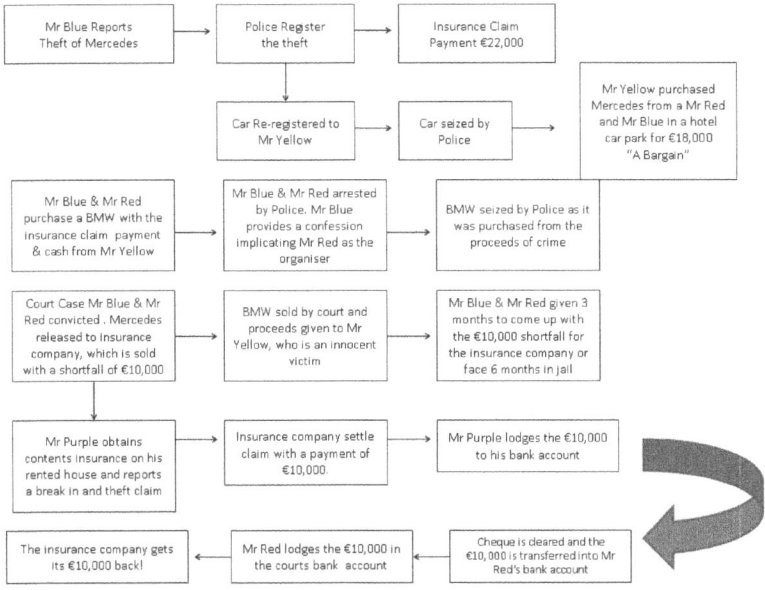

This case was given the nickname "Sweet and Sour" by the investigators, as it was all going well, until the Police Detectives traced the property claim payment back to the insurance company. Effectively the insurance company received the €10,000 which was their own money returning via a suspected false property insurance claim.

Motor Injury Fraud

As there are so many different entities and parties involved, this makes the investigation of road traffic accident insurance claims by far the most difficult and complex. Take,

Universal Scams & Fraud Detection

for example, two cars colliding on a road with multiple occupants who all sustain personal injury. From the two cars, you may have nine individual personal injury claims, which could range from minor cuts and abrasions to serious life-threatening injuries.

Investigating one of these claims can be difficult and time consuming. It is imperative that the insurance investigator gets access to the files as soon as possible as like fire claim investigations, evidence erodes with the passing of time.

The investigator will need to work closely with the internal specialist claims team handlers and also external suppliers such as Motor Assessors and Forensic vehicle and accident Investigators, who examine the scene of the accident and the vehicles involved. This helps with the determining liability for the accident. It is also critical that the insurance investigator views the location of the accident, identifies and interviews obtaining statements from any potential witnesses.

One of the key requirements of the insurance investigator is attention to detail whilst investigating. Sometimes a seemingly minor detail can turn into the missing piece of the puzzle. Taking of notes is important along with constantly reviewing and updating them. As the investigation progresses all new information obtained needs to be examined for evidential value.

When investigating injury insurance claims, the insurance investigator should also keep in mind, the possibility that the accident may have been staged. The term "staged" accident is a planned or acted accident. An example would be the driver of the insured vehicle may well be in collusion with the driver and or passengers of the other vehicles. These accidents are normally at low velocity with minimal damage and in some cases no damage to the accident vehicles.

One practice of organised fraudulent traffic accidents is known as 'Crash for Cash'. These claims are planned and orchestrated by criminals in order to profit from the insurance compensation. A financial debt may be outstanding to a criminal by an ordinary decent citizen who has fallen on hard times. The criminal will arrange for the citizen to crash into another vehicle, one with maximum occupants. Any payment for compensation to the passengers of the cars is then collected by the criminal.

The unlucky Roundabout

One particular roundabout in the UK was the subject of many road traffic accidents involving cars with multiple occupants.

Universal Scams & Fraud Detection

The accidents were staged and part of an elaborate crash for cash scam. The individual, Mr Mohammed Patel, would drive his car in front of an unwitting motorist. He would suddenly and without reason slam on the brakes causing the person travelling behind him to crash into him. He would then file a claim for personal injury against the insurance company of the unfortunate motorist. In total, Mr Patel had 93 accidents on the roundabout, generating sterling £1.6 million in insurance claims.

However office workers who worked in the vicinity of the roundabout became suspicious of the number of accidents and reported the incidents to the Police. The UK's Insurance Fraud Bureau working with the Police put together an elaborate surveillance operation and eventually arrested Mr Patel who was subsequently convicted and jailed. In summing up Judge Bernard Lever advised "This kind of fraud is costing the UK industry £1.9 billion and this adds, we are told, about £49 to every single motorist's insurance premium."

EMPLOYERS / PUBLIC LIABILITY FRAUD

A former Irish Tánaiste (Deputy Prime Minister) stated "the high cost of insurance was putting jobs at risk and jeopardised the country's competitiveness."

Insurance Fraud

There is no doubt that the cost of Employers' and Public Liability has a direct effect on unemployment. After all, the cost of insurance is a key factor in any budgeting plans that a company must undertake when forecasting the operating cost of the business. Much has been done in Ireland to reduce the cost of insurance. The introduction of the Civil Liability and Courts Act which greatly assists in the defence of false insurance claims. In particular, section 26 addresses fraudulent evidence in personal injury claims. If a person provides false evidence then the court can dismiss the action.

It is crucial for any organisation to have a robust plan in operation for dealing with all insurance claims. The threat of fraud is ever present and a possibility in all claims, so it is vital that all employers and employees cooperate with the insurance companies investigation in their efforts to prevent fraud.

All staff should be made aware of the high cost associated with insurance and the importance of protection against suspect claims. Any slips, trips or falls by employees or members of the public must be reported to management and recorded, for example, in an accident report book. The company should also take photographs if possible and obtain the name address and contact phone numbers of any potential witnesses. Preservation of any potential evidence is also crucial, in particular CCTV footage. The insurance investigator will look for this information whilst investigating the claim.

The Irish fast food chain Supermac's was one of the first companies to publicise the issue of false public liability claims. CCTV footage, capturing individuals pouring water on a bathroom floor before slipping on the water and sustaining alledged personal injury is one of the classics. This video evidence demonstrates the challenges faced by businesses in preventing these fraudulent claims.

When a claim is dismissed as being fraudulent, insurance companies and the self-insured, must pursue the claimants for the costs associated in investigating and defending the claim. There should be no "having a free go" when it comes to fraudulent insurance claims. The cost of false Employee and Public Liability insurance claims is passed onto the consumer in the form of increased premiums. It is every policy holder who pays for the cost of the fraud. The business or company, in turn has to build this cost into the price of their product or service.

When investigating and defending an Employees' or Public Liability insurance claim, a well-written accident report form is of great benefit. The following details should be included in the form:

Insurance Fraud

Injured Person:

First Name

Surname

Date of Birth

Contact Phone Number

Email Address

Part of Body injured

Employee / Contractor / Visitor / Other

_____

Incident Details:

Date & time of Incident

Location of incident

Full Details of the accident

Details of equipment being used

If outside, weather at time

Record of injuries sustained

Universal Scams & Fraud Detection

EMERGENCY RESPONSE:

First Responder details
___

Security Officer Details
___

Did Police Attend / Details
___

Ambulance Details
___

___

EVIDENCE PRESERVATION:

CCTV footage removed for preservation
___

___

Report on CCTV footage, including time on recoding
___

___

Witness names, contact details (not mobile numbers)
___

___

Photograph scene of accident, attach to report
___

___

Warning signs in place
___

___

Insurance Fraud

HEALTH & SAFETY CONSIDERATIONS

Any equipment being used at time of accident

_____

_____

Safety equipment being used at time of accident

_____

_____

Lighting & Noise levels at time of accident

_____

_____

Maintenance records of any machinery

_____

_____

If Visitor injured, record of pass issued

_____

_____

HR (EMPLOYEE ACCIDENTS)

Training Records of injured in place

_____

_____

Record of absence following accident

_____

_____

HR file in place and preserved

_____

_____

OTHER CONSIDERATIONS:

Is there a need to report to the Health & Safety Authority?
_____

_____

Insurance Company or Broker informed?
_____

_____

Is there a need to make changes following the accident?
_____

_____

INVESTIGATION:

Written Statements of witnesses
_____

_____

Sketch and / or Photographs of the accident locus
_____

_____

All evidence secured for future needs
_____

_____

Investigator's Name & Signature
_____

_____

Date Report Completed (as soon after incident is best practice)
_____

Insurance Fraud

Original Report held with Health & Safety, copied to HR and Directors.

It is also most important that the above along with any evidence from the date of the accident is preserved as it will be of evidential value.

JEWELLERY CLAIMS FRAUD

Jewellery claims are generally high-volume claims which require specialised investigation. Such claims are typically outsourced to specialist loss adjusters, trained in the identification and valuation of jewellery.

It is inevitable that, with the ease with which jewellery can be sold to pawn brokers and on the black market, individuals might be tempted to sell items and then claim their theft.

One particular case involved the theft of valuable Rolex watch. As is the common practice, the appointed loss adjuster requested proof of ownership. In the absence of a receipt for purchase, the claimant provided the original Rolex box in which the watch was supplied. However the box was supplied on the condition that it would be returned to the claimant.

Universal Scams & Fraud Detection

However the same loss adjuster was investigating a second claim for the loss of a Rolex and once again a box was supplied. On this occasion the adjuster placed a small pen mark on the box before returning.

(Bottom right of white box) A couple of weeks passed and the Loss Adjuster received a claim from yet another insured. Once again, a Rolex Box was produced as evidence of ownership. It was the same box with the identification mark. The matter was passed to the police for investigation.

When we consider insurance fraud, we mainly think of fraudulent claims. However, there is also the practice of fraud at the underwriting stage which also affects the cost of insurance. When completing an insurance proposal form or requesting a quote of insurance cover, it is important to always tell the full truth. It is also vital to take nothing for granted.

Insurance Fraud

NON-DISCLOSURE OF INFORMATION / FALSE DECLARATIONS

Non-disclosure of information that could affect the issuing of the contract of insurance is a very serious matter. Take for example an individual who fails to disclose previous insurance claims or an individual who fails to disclose that they have criminal convictions. If this information comes to light at the time of a claim, the policy of insurance may be voided, leaving the individual in a difficult position. It may well not have been the individual's intention to deceive, but 'intention' generally is not considered and the policy will still be cancelled.

The Insurance industry now has IT tools, used to check if a claimant has had previous claims which were not disclosed. In Ireland, the Insurance Link system is used for sharing claims data between insurers. In North America ISO provides the IT system and in the UK, Claims and Underwriting Exchange CUE provides the system along with other IT platforms for sharing of claims specific data.

SAME CLAIM, DIFFERENT ADDRESS:

One particular individual insured his house advising that he had no previous insurance claims. A few months later, his house was burgled and he placed a claim valued at €40,000 with his insurance company. The insurance investigator ran the insured address through the Insurance Link database and found no previous claims for the address. However when he ran the insured's name and date of birth he found a claims match eighteen months previously, for another address. Further investigation revealed that the insured had an almost identical claim for burglary from another insurer, receiving a compensation payment of €15,700. As this information was not disclosed at the policy inception, the insurance policy was deemed void.

FRONTING:

If you are young enough to remember trying to insure your first car, the cost of which was more than the car was worth, then we are from the same generation. In 1989 I was quoted the equivalent of €1,500 for an 850cc Austin Mini worth €500. Thankfully, things have improved since then, with the cost of obtaining insurance for younger first time drivers drastically reduced. "Fronting" is a practice where, in order to secure a lower premium, somebody, who is not the main user of a vehicle states that they are, and then adds the car's principle user as a "named driver" on the policy.

The risk is significantly higher on a less experienced driver in comparison to the more experienced person. Insurance quotations are based on the technical pricing of the potential risk.

Insurance Fraud

Obviously there are more accidents based on inexperience, which can be extremely costly to individuals lives and insurance pay-outs.

PREMIUM FRAUD:

Premium fraud is the embezzlement or diversion of the money paid by an individual to a third party such as a fake broker. This is known as Ghost Broking. Insurance companies and their intermediates are licensed to operate as financial institution by government authorities. If using a third party to obtain insurance, it is advisable to ensure that this party is licensed to practise.

Premium fraud is more common in the Unites States then in Europe, but there is risk of being a victim of premium fraud closer to home. In fact, there was one case in which an individual posed to be from a large British Insurance company newly operating in Ireland. He was selling reduced cost motor insurance policies. The individual had manufactured a false identity card and obtained forged policy documentation. This individual then tried to sell false policies to innocent consumers. However the scam was prevented by Detectives from the Irish police specialists, National Bureau of Criminal Investigation. The Detectives worked undercover, posing as potential customers. The individual sold a false policy and was subsequently arrested.

Universal Scams & Fraud Detection

GENERAL ADVICE FOR CONSUMERS

- Any suspect insurance claims should be reported to the local Police, insurance company or industry bodies such as those listed below.
- If involved in a road traffic accident, note the identities of all occupants in the other vehicles and if possible the position in which they were sitting in the other vehicle.
- Photographs should be taken of the accident scene. Use your mobile phone camera or ask a witness to take photographs.
- The accident should be reported to the Police. It is also advisable to obtain a police identification report number. (In Ireland, known as a PULSE number)
- Try and locate any witnesses and request contact details in including a landline phone number.
- Written valuations and photographs of insurable items should be obtained, the details of which should be listed with your insurance company.
- Work-place accidents should be reported to the Security or Health & Safety officer as soon as possible.
- When obtaining an insurance policy, check that you have supplied all information requested and that the information supplied is correct and accurate.

Insurance Fraud

LINKS TO INSURANCE FRAUD PREVENTION IN SPECIFIC COUNTRIES:

www.insuranceconfidential.ie	Ireland
www.insurancefraud.org	USA
www.insurancefraudbureau.org	UK
www.ifba.org.au	Australia
www.ibc.ca	Canada
www.saicb.co.za	South Africa

{14}

Banks, Credit Cards & Cybercrime

"I rob banks for a living, what do you do?"
John Dillinger- Bank Robber USA

There are many ways of defrauding a bank, which are detailed in the diagram below. Like insurance companies, banks need to cover the cost of fraud and, once again the cost is covered by the honest customer. All banks have recruited fraud prevention managers, investigators and IT support staff. However, individuals continue to attempt to defraud banks, crimes which are less risky and more profitable than armed hold-ups. Let's now take a closer look at some of the key risks which banks face, on local, national and global scales.

Mortgage Fraud & Lending Fraud:

Mortgage and Lending fraud is similar to Insurance Application Fraud, or non- disclosure of material facts during the application process. It normally is perpetrated by individuals working in partnership with a lawyer or accountant. Like other types of fraud it is difficult to detect as minimal information is available about the customer at application stage. Having the ability of quotation enrichment, is the most common form of investigation available to the financial institution. Using data analytics, predictive analysis and examination of the provided data, permits lenders to verify or gain a greater understanding of the applicants true financial status.

Common forms of mortgage fraud would include:
- Obtaining multiple mortgages from different banks and lenders on a single property, by forgery of land registry documents.
- Gross exaggeration of earnings or income
- Hiding of outgoings such as child maintenance, or another mortgage
- The over valuation of the property
- Obtaining a mortgage by way of the identity theft of a deceased or living person.
- Non-disclosure of other relevant facts or being scarce with the truth, such as rent earned on a rented property.

According to a recent survey in the UK, there has been a 23% rise in attempted mortgage fraud, detected and prevented at application stage. The main reason for this detection is the closer scrutiny of lenders, caused by current economic situation. The Company Experian provide anti-fraud application, fraud detection software and advise that 39 out of every 10,000 mortgage applications are found to be fraudulent. The vast majority of the detections related to individuals dishonesty about earnings.

Universal Scams & Fraud Detection

CARD OR PLASTIC FRAUD:

Credit cards and their use have evolved over the last twenty years. With the development of the internet our financial transactions have changed. For example we no longer go to the travel agency to book a flight. This has become an ever-simple internet transaction. Ryanair has become Europe's largest airline, largely by selling almost every ticket via the internet.

The development of Kindle books, holiday-bookings or purchases on Amazon, the availability of instant credit, security and ease of use, has made credit card purchases a distinct advantage over cash transactions. This will continue with the development of the internet. According to industry sources Credit Card fraud is now costing globally almost US$14 billion a year with United States of America accounting for 51% of the total cost. Europol advises that credit card fraud is costing €1.3 billion a year in Europe. It is also, globally, a growing problem.

Fraudsters have also evolved. Using a stolen credit card to make a card-not-present (CNP) transaction over the internet has never been easier. Chip-And-Pin has been successful in reducing fraud in Europe, but this only works in a retail transaction environment. Card-not-present continues to be a significant problem for credit card providers. Banks are combating CNP with the deployment of 3D Secure. This validates the identity of the card user by asking a security question, before authorising payment.

How many of us get our monthly credit card statement and actually take a few minutes to analyse the transactions. Most credit card thefts involve a small purchase perhaps a couple of euro or dollars, before trying a larger transaction. Banks use various IT tools to monitor the daily transactions of their customers. A strange or out of character transaction will trigger an alert, which suspends or questions the transaction. The bank fraud office will make contact with the card owner. If the transaction cannot be authenticated the bank will refuse authorisation and instruct the customer to destroy the card. But we can all play a part in preventing credit card fraud. By checking statements and immediately alerting the bank of any suspicious activity can dramatically reduce the success rate of the credit card fraudsters.

Universal Scams & Fraud Detection

LESSONS LEARNED – PROTECTING YOUR PLASTIC:

1- Online purchases should only be made from reputable websites, with secure (https) domains
2- Offers by website to 'Store Information' should be declined
3- Credit card statements should be examined for unknown or suspicious transactions. Statements should be stored in a secure location or shredded before disposal
4- Credit cards should not be let out of sight. The location of some chip-and-pin machines have deemed it necessary for cards to be taken out of a customers' proximity. If this happens you should go with the salesperson to the machine
5- Conceal your pin and be alert to suspect signs such as camera's or loose keypads at the ATM
6- Talk to your bank – If going abroad or making a large out of the ordinary purchase, alert your bank
7- Keep your Credit card secure and ensure your personal identification number (PIN) is not written down

Banks, Credit Cards & Cybercrime

CYBERCRIME:

There are many definitions for Cyber Crime, but I prefer the simple *'Any criminal act using a computer and the Internet'*. State, national laws and enforcement agencies have boundaries. The internet and cybercrime does not have the same boundaries and is effectively a global phenomenon. It is possible for young 'whiz kids' or a hacking expert to access, from his bedroom, a financial institutions IT system. In hacking circles, this can be seen as a badge of honour, but causes serious embarrassment to the financial organisation under attack.

We also need to be mindful of terrorist cyber-criminals who are intent of obtaining financial gain for supporting their terrorism. According to Interpol, Cyber-crime, including identity theft and child pornography, accounts for some of the fastest growing criminality in the world.

Having attended the European Middle East and African (EMEA) conference of the International Association of Financial Crime Investigators in Amsterdam, it was revealed that Cyber-crime is a major concern for financial industries and nationals security agencies. Attempted attacks on financial industries IT systems are on the rise, the results of which understandably, if successful, can cause havoc.

Universal Scams & Fraud Detection

Financial institutions spend vast amounts investing in IT security systems. However, staff and customers must also be involved in preventing cyber fraud by simple means such as protecting their system passwords and being aware of suspect emails which may contain Trojans or malware. There is also a need to educate staff and customers from phishing exercises, looking for personal security information and or passwords.

There are three key reasons for the growth of cybercrime. First, with the ever increasing scale and popularity of the internet, in particular social media, there is an ongoing surge of personal information available. Second, the anonymity of the cybercriminal operating from a remote location and thirdly, the difficulty faced by investigators and law enforcement with multi jurisdiction investigations. All of these factors contribute to the ever growing threat of cybercrime.

One of the most infamous cyber-crimes, involving identity theft, credit card fraud, money laundering and terrorist financing, involved the massive international investigation by the United States and the UK's SO 15 Anti Terrorism Unit. Three terrorists Tarig Al-Daour, Younis Tsouli and Waseem Mughal, all pleaded guilty to terrorism in the UK. According to the Washington Post the men laundered funds from stolen credit cards through online gambling websites. The leader of the group, Tarig Al-Daour, had in his possession a computer

Banks, Credit Cards & Cybercrime

with 37,000 compromised credit card numbers and the true card holders addresses, dates of birth and approximate balance on the cards. Using these stolen identities, these individuals made purchases of airline tickets and mobile cell phones. A shopping list was also found which included GPS satellite positioning systems, night vision goggles and survival knives. There were also internet websites registered, inciting terrorism and one even showed how to make a bomb vest for a suicide bombing attack. All three received lengthy jail sentences in the UK.

The Judge hearing the case remarked " The trouble is I don't understand the language. I don't really understand what a website is." This is a perfect example of the complexity of cyber-crime and the struggle faced by the Security Services and financial institutions. It is also the clearest indicator of all that financial institutions need to retain professional IT security and train their own staff.

Lessons Learned:

- ✓ The services of a professional IT security company should be retained.
- ✓ Educate your staff and customers on Cybercrime and the ever present threat
- ✓ Have IT security in place and updated to prevent virus attacks, malware etc., run regular scans on the systems and computers.
- ✓ Ensure staff change passwords a minimum of once a month. This should include Cloud systems and USB memory sticks.
- ✓ Social Media, make staff aware of the dangers of supplying company and personal data on these websites
- ✓ Backup important data and have emergency contact numbers for IT company.

Banks, Credit Cards & Cybercrime

Fraud Prevention Strategy:

When drafting a fraud prevention strategy, for a financial institution we should consider all ways to mitigate the risk and loss. In addition we should also consider the customer and reputation of the organisation. However by adopting these key points, the risk will be reduced.

Key Mitigating Factors:

- ✓ Top down approach to combating fraud
- ✓ All staff should be enabled and empowered to have a duty to protect the company
- ✓ Set the standard of a Zero tolerance of fraud within the organisation
- ✓ Training for all staff on fraud awareness
- ✓ Public Awareness campaign, documents and web site (liaise with Marketing)
- ✓ Full participation with industry groups and regular meetings with law enforcement. Be aware of current trends and issues facing all within the industry
- ✓ Open Door policy to fraud – Staff free to raise concerns, a confidential phone hotline to management

Mitigation Filtration Triangle

A top-down approach, from the CEO or President of the organisation to the customer, will permit and empower staff and customers alike to be constantly aware and vigilant to the ever present threat.

Implementation of Strategy

Recognising and mitigating the risk, it is critical to implement a strategy to prevent and detect attacks by criminals. This strategy must be fully documented and easily implementable in a timely and cost effective manner. However it is pointless and useless to have strategy documents if you do not investigate suspicious activity.

The ADID system, detailed below will prove effective if implemented by a team of fully-trained and experienced fraud investigators, who are encouraged to liaise with the organisation's senior management.

Avoid

The overall goal and strategy should be to prevent fraud from occurring by implementing procedures and fraud prevention software, such as Experian Hunter, ISO or Risk Intelligence.

Detect

Detection of suspicious activity, reported immediately to the fraud investigation team.

Investigate

Professional investigation, preservation of evidence and liaison with local law enforcement.

Deter

Always assist the police with the prosecution of fraudsters. Publicise fraud results, which should be managed and working in tandem with the marketing department.

{15}

Car Scams

"BMW 320i for Sale, low mileage, like new perfect condition, only one owner from new, never crashed, quick sale owner emigrating, hence low price"

This was an online car sale advertisement and included photographs placed on the internet. The advertisement read and looked right and raised the interest of many potential purchasers. The true details of the car were not included in the advertisement for obvious reasons – that it had been previously written-off in a serious road traffic accident. It also had triple the recorded mileage, had a number of previous owners and had been imported from another country. Thankfully the deception was spotted by a potential buyer, who reported their concerns to the police. Detectives commenced an investigation, resulting in the vehicle being seized. There are, however, thousands of second-hand vehicles purchased every year in Ireland without any background checks by the purchasers.

When purchasing a car, it is imperative to carry out checks on the history of the vehicle, even if purchasing from a reputable dealer. There are services, such as Cartel or Mywheels. ie, who supply a full history of any vehicle. It is also advisable to employ a professional motor assessor to inspect the vehicle for defects, mileage abnormalities and signs of previous damage repairs. The vast majority of people selling cars are honest but there are that few who will sell a damaged or stolen vehicle without any concerns for the innocent purchaser.

Typical Car Selling Scams:

Clocking: Reducing the mileage / kilometres recorded on the speedometer. An incentive for the purchaser to buy the vehicle with less mileage. This can be checked against service records and looking for above average wear on the brake and clutch pedals.

Finance Outstanding: Selling a car in which a bank or other financial lending institution still holds an interest in the vehicle. Individuals have been caught out buying a vehicle and then the vehicle is repossessed by a company. It is always advisable

Car Scams

to run a check for finance outstanding on the vehicle before making the purchase.

Middlemen: It is advisable not to buy a second hand car from an individual representing the owner of the car. These middlemen will take a deposit or in some cases the full amount whilst the deal is finalised and then simply disappear.

Internet Scams: We should be extra vigilant when buying a high value item online. One fraud involved a person selling a high spec luxury car as they had moved out of the country. The price quoted seemed too good to be true. Without seeing the car, the unfortunate purchaser lodged money to a bank account as a deposit payment. The car never materialised and the purchaser had no recourse.

Vehicles with a History: Cars sold as never being involved in a previous accident. However when examined by a Motor Engineer it becomes apparent that the car has been involved in an accident and repaired. Using companies like My Wheels.ie or Cartel can help prevent you purchasing a previously damaged car.

Fake Bank Drafts: Another problem involves selling the car to an individual who supplies you with a bank draft. On occasions bank drafts are forged documents, when presented at a bank they are considered worthless. They should be treated like a cheque. If somebody wants to pay you with a bank draft then you should first present the bank draft at a bank and have it cleared into your bank account before handing over your car.

Cloning: A vehicle is stolen to order, why? Cars that have been involved in serious accidents are written off by the insurance company. This leaves the salvage of the vehicle sold at an auction, normally for a low amount as the vehicle should not be put back on the road. The criminal will then seek to steal an identical vehicle, i.e. same model, make and colour possibly even year of manufacturer. They will then clone the second vehicle with the identity of the vehicle that has been previously written off. If a Police officer stops the vehicle and runs a check on the registration then the vehicle will match the registration, making it difficult to prevent this crime from occurring.

Remember like other scams, if the asking price is too good to be true, then most likely it is too good to be true!

THE VAN WITH A HISTORY:

Insurance companies have been investigating a scam in Ireland and other countries which involves the importation of vehicles with a history in another country. An insurance claim I investigated involved an individual who filed a claim for his commercial vehicle, which he allegedly crashed. The claim was suspect and was investigated. According to the man he was tired and simply lost concentration crashing into a large wall on a dark country road. The damage on the vehicle and the wall was consistent with a collision.

However, upon realising that the vehicle was imported from the UK, a Motor Industry Anti-Fraud Theft Register (MIAFTR) check revealed that the same vehicle had been involved in a road traffic accident six months earlier and written off by a UK insurer. Photographs from the UK insurance company confirmed the same damage and the claim was declined. The matter was referred to the Gardai and the individual was subsequently prosecuted.

Which car is yours?

Another suspect insurance claim involved a BMW that had been crashed and sustained severe damage. The insurance company engaged the services of a motor assessor who inspected the vehicle which determined that the car was imported into Ireland, but the chassis belonged to a completely different car. When the chassis numbers were checked, they revealed that both vehicles had been written off in the UK and the salvage of both were assembled into one car in Ireland. When this information was put to the insured, the claim was withdrawn and the matter was referred to the Gardai.

Universal Scams & Fraud Detection

Robbery

A more sinister crime, involves the theft of money and threatened violence when attempting to purchase a car. An individual agrees to purchase a vehicle with cash and to meet the seller at a discrete location. On arrival, the customer is robbed at knife or gun point. To date, this crime has only been committed by one perpetrator or gang who have not been caught.

With private car sales, cash transactions should be avoided. Bank transfers and online payments such as PayPal should be utilised. If meeting to exchange goods and payment, meetings should be in a public location, preferable at locations with CCTV coverage.

Letterbox Fishing

Most main car brands advise that the car cannot be stolen without the keys. Modern vehicles have a digital immobiliser fitted into the key which communicates with the car engine. If the key is not present the car engine will not start.

How many of us come into our homes from a hard day's work and leave our keys on the hall table? Criminals know this and are using fishing rods and litter pickers or grabbers to fish the keys out through the letterboxes. Having the keys for the vehicle will defeat vehicle security mechanisms and permit the criminal to simply drive away with your car. In addition, the resulting difficulty to prove the theft may complicate an insurance claim.

Car Scams

An Unfortunate Job:

A young Irishman who was unemployed saw an advertisement on the internet looking for a part-time car sales courier. He applied for the job, met with his employer in a hotel and was immediately offered the position. As part of his trial period he was handed an envelope containing a bankers draft and told to drive to the West of Ireland to collect a car and hand over the banker's draft. Little does he know, he is a pawn in an elaborate scam.

The man's employer had agreed a €10,000 price (lower then the car's true value to ensure a quick sale) over the phone and had despatched his new employee to complete the transaction. A deal was negotiated with the seller of the car who agreed to accept a bank draft in payment for the vehicle. While this is happening the employer places an advertisement on the internet for the sale of the newly purchased car at a much lower price of €5,000.

The transaction is completed with the handing over of a bank draft. Normally the deal is arranged for a Friday afternoon so the seller misses the bank closing time.

The employee is told by his employer to hold onto the car for the weekend as a little perk of the job. However on the Sunday morning, the employee is told to go to a hotel. He meets with a man who buys the car for €5,000 cash. The new employee then meets with his employer and hands over the €5,000.

The following day the employee carries out another similar courier sale involving a bank draft, quick car sale and once again hands over the money to his employer.

The employee has been concerned; he hears nothing from his new employer. He is infinitely shocked when he was questioned by Garda Detectives and told that his employer is a clever conman, buying cars with false bank drafts. Selling them on for cash and distancing himself from the actual transactions by using unknowing messengers, who innocently hand over the ill-gotten gains.

To date the conman behind this elaborate fraud has not been brought to justice.

When buying a car you should consider the following pointers:

- ✓ Is the price offered the true car's value? Check similar model prices online and with dealers.
- ✓ Be wary of emotional pleas, such as the owner mentioning the fact they are emigrating, hence low price.
- ✓ The vehicle should be viewed during the day, so light is not an issue.

Car Scams

- ✓ The Vehicle Licensing Certificate (VLC) / Registration Certificate should be confirmed as genuine. Genuine documents will include watermarks. If unsure check with law enforcement before making the purchase.
- ✓ Brake and clutch pedals should be checked for signs of wear, inconsistent with the vehicles mileage.
- ✓ The service history of the car should be checked for inconsistency.
- ✓ The vehicle identification number (VIN) on the engine should be checked for any sign of tampering.
- ✓ Doors, windows, boot and surrounding areas to be checked for damage, suggesting break-in.
- ✓ An online search, using MyWheels, Cartel etc., of the vehicle's registration history should be checked.
- ✓ The Insurance Disc, tax cert and NCT cert should be confirmed as valid and associated with the car.
- ✓ If the registration plates are newer than the car, a satisfactory reason should be secured before a sale is agreed.
- ✓ The keys provided for the car should be inspected, how many keys are issued for the car, how many should there be, do all keys start the car engine, open doors and boot.
- ✓ The identity of the seller should be confirmed – proof of identity including postal address should be asked for, a mobile phone number and/or email address should not suffice as they cannot be used to track down a seller.

Universal Scams & Fraud Detection

- ✓ A qualified vehicle Assessor should be retained to inspect the vehicle before any sale is finalised..
- ✓ Advertisements asking to call between specific hours, e.g. 7-8pm should be considered with suspicion, as they could be using a public telephone.
- ✓ The seller should be met at their home, to confirm address of the car's registration and matched against the vehicle Licensing Certificate
- ✓ The buyer should be aware that a car that has been previously stolen will be returned to its rightful owner. The buyer will lose the car and the money paid for it.

{16}

Fraud against the Elderly

> *"Youth is wasted on the young"*
> Oscar Wilde

Whilst carrying out research for this chapter, I found some of my findings personally disturbing and somewhat disgusting. Fraud against a financial institution is almost anticipated or expected. However fraud against elderly people, who are targeted solely based on their age and on the possibility that, over their lives, they have accumulated significant savings, is one the most shameful crimes. These vulnerable people need to be protected. Elderly people contribute to our society in many ways, in particular by talking of their experience and knowledge of years past, which in turn enriches the youth of today.

Universal Scams & Fraud Detection

The con artist will think nothing of applying their evil trade in order to gain the confidence of elderly people and relieve them of savings and investments. It is additionally disturbing to note that these scams occasionally include intimidation and even violence.

We all have a duty to protect the elderly and should always make it our business to check in with elderly people living in our neighbourhood. We should also give consideration to the current elderly generation, who are not familiar with computers and the internet. Banking, obtaining revenue forms and insurance online is now considered normal practice, however this creates difficulty to some of the elderly who may appreciate support.

According to the Federal Bureau of Investigation (FBI) elderly people are less likely to report being the victims of fraud, as they simply don't know who to report the scam. In some cases they are ashamed and concerned that relatives may think they are no longer fit to take care of themselves and may feel isolated. It is also widely accepted that, in some cases, elderly people do not make good witnesses and do not want the pressure and stress of giving evidence in court. This is also known by the con artist who exploits their vulnerability. It is important that organisations such as the Citizens' Advice Bureau provide information and resources to elderly

Fraud against the Elderly

people, offering advice on how to avoid being conned, how to act if approached by a suspicious individual and who to contact in the event of falling victim to a fraudster.

It is interesting and appalling to learn that in many cases, fraud against an elderly person is committed by a relative and or care-giver. This can be a difficult fraud to detect and investigate as financial transactions on behalf of the elderly person may well appear legitimate, even when investigated. The victim will be particularly afraid or ashamed to report the fraud by a relative. They may even feel isolated and lonely.

Fraud against an elderly person by a relative or care-giver might manifest itself in the following ways:
- The Relative or care-giver taking a higher than expected interest in the person's financial affairs.
- Shortage of food, hygiene or other personal items for the person
- Utility bills not paid by the carer, when they have been authorised to do so. Services (phone, TV etc.) being discontinued.
- Purchases made on behalf of the person, for which they have no need or interest.
- The person's normal bank account or, credit card, changed to another bank in which they have no previous history or relationship, without just cause or reason.

Universal Scams & Fraud Detection

If any of the above signs are present and even if a reasonable explanation is provided by the carer or relative, it would be prudent to contact another family member or, if none available, seek legal advice.

TELEMARKETING FRAUD:

A telephone gives an elderly person a sense of security, especially if they live by themselves. A key fraud threat to the elderly is Telemarketing fraud. According to the United States Bureau of Consumer Protection, telemarketing fraud costs approximately US$40 billion a year, with the victims in their retirement years being in the majority. Scammers obtain the phone numbers of the individuals and hone in on them, offering them special and unique offers. They work on the confidence trick and know that the older person has time to talk and may be too polite to hang up the phone. One tried and tested con is the 'once in a lifetime offer', an offer of an inexpensive item or service that must be availed of immediately. Applying light pressure not to 'miss out' is often enough to make them part with their money.

The term "Robo-calls" is used to describe computer auto-dialler telephone scammers who repeatedly call with an "offer" for the occupant and asking for personal details 'necessary to process' the order or prize. They are simply phising exercises made in the hope that the person will release valuable

Fraud against the Elderly

identity information, such as credit card details or social security numbers.

There are some basic rules or guidelines that we can follow to protect the elderly from telemarking fraud:
- If you didn't enter a draw then how can you have won a prize?
- Under no circumstances should personal information be shared with any person not completely trusted. If asked for such information, take the caller's contact details and inform a relative or care-giver.
- Calls coming in after business hours should raise additional suspicion.
- Callers applying undue pressure should raise concern.
- It is acceptable to simply hang up if a caller is unknown, asking inappropriate questions or simply raising suspicion. If possible record the date and time of the call and pass to a relative or care-giver.

Any suspicion that an elderly person is being conned should be reported. Consider the following points:
- The local law enforcement authority should be informed and an incident number taken.
- Obtain a Financial Credit check on the person, using Experian or the Irish Credit Bureau.

Universal Scams & Fraud Detection

- If there is suspected unauthorised activity on an elderly person's bank account or credit card, the bank should be contacted and account statements requested.
- Check the statements for any unknown or out of the ordinary purchases
- Ensure the letter box has not been tampered with to make sure no unauthorised person can access the post.
- Check with the local Post Office in respect of any delivery of unsolicited mail or parcels to the address. Consider the possibility of the identity theft of the elderly person.
- Computers used by an elderly person should be checked, ensuring adequate virus and email protection

COLD CALLING TO THE HOME:

The pre-cursor to the telephone con, the cold call, involved the con-artist knocking on an elderly person's door offering a deal or prize, with the intention of eliciting personal details or gaining access to the person's home. The scammers are once again phising for information and trying to gain access to the person's property. It is important that there is adequate physical security, front doors should be fitted with a chain lock.

THE BUILDER SCAM:

An extension of the cold call, this involves a man knocking on the door, advising that he is a builder working in the area and that he spotted a cracked slate or other damage on the roof,

Fraud against the Elderly

which he will fix for a small amount of money. Then, whilst repairing the slate he finds more damage and offers to repair them for a higher amount. It is unlikely the elderly person will be able to confirm that the repairs are needed and may agree, especially if the 'builder' applies pressure, suggesting possible roof leaks if not repaired. Other scams may include someone who is cleaning gutters and state that they have observed similar damage whilst up the ladder.

Terrified of the bank collapse:

A 70 year old man who withdrew his savings of almost €30,000 which he had saved to cover his routine costs and his funeral/burial was robbed by a man posing as a member of the Gardai (Irish police). The conman informed the elderly man that the bank was going to collapse and that he would take care of his savings. The Judge described the case as "a very mean crime against a vulnerable old man." There have been other cases of conmen posing as members of the Police or other officials. If in doubt you should call your local police station to verify the identity of the officer.

Lessons Learned

- ✓ Never pay on the promise that you have won a prize
- ✓ Any person calling to your home, should be asked for an identity card with a photograph. If not satisfied, the person should not be allowed enter. If the person does not leave, the occupant should close the door, contact a friend or the authorities
- ✓ Personal information, especially regarding identity should be protected
- ✓ Individuals making unsolicited visits, offering services such as building work, should not be entertained
- ✓ Services should not be paid for in cash, especially if the service provider is insisting on an immediate cash payment
- ✓ If getting work done, ensure that the service provider is reputable, always check references

{17}

Internet Dating - Love Rats

"It's like the Wild West, the Internet. There are no rules."
Steven Wright

Would you like to dance? I am old enough to remember the days of standing in the local night club, in my case Tamango's located in North Dublin, mustering up the courage to ask some lady up to dance. This would now appear to be no longer the case. With the evolution of the social networking and dating websites, there is now a safer way to get dates and find love. Or perhaps not.

Single people looking for love, especially lonely people desperate for love, are susceptible to charm and flattery and therefore, are easy prey for a con-artist.

Universal Scams & Fraud Detection

There is no denying it, love is a wonderful thing. When we meet someone and fall in love, we readily let our defences down and ignore voices in our heads, telling us that all may not be what it seems.

It is important to note from the outset that the majority of people using online dating, internet chat rooms and social networking are genuine people searching for a partner and friendship. But these con-men know to use all of these tactics as they hunt for the next prey. According to sources, divorced and widowed women over the age of 40 are most at risk. The con-man will send a complimentary, charming and witty email to a susceptible individual showing that he is keen that they get to know each other. Many emails and some photographs will be exchanged during this grooming period.

The personal details and photographs provided by the con-man will, of course, be fake and the email address untraceable. Just because you are communicating with someone who describes themselves as 25 years of age, 6ft tall, works out in the gym and looks like a lifeguard from Baywatch, that may not be the case. It is a simple exercise to set up a fake generic email address, then select and copy someone's photograph from the internet to their false social media profile.

Internet Dating - Love Rats

There is a chance you could be dealing with a fake persona and especially worrying if you have a teenage daughter. This is also a notorious ploy used by cybersex predators, potentially looking to prey on innocent children.

Having been suitably charming and attentive, the con artist will have groomed you to obtain your confidence and may ask you to deposit money in a particular bank account or provide your address to accept some post from them. This is con-artists way of obtaining valuable information about your identity. There is a certain perception of safety when we're at home with the doors locked but, by going online, we might be exposing just as much as we would by leaving our front door wide open and our money and personal documents on the front step.

At all times you should maintain your caution whilst engaging with internet conversation and also ensure that you have updated internet virus protection.

According to the UK's National Fraud Intelligence Bureau, online dating is becoming more socially acceptable and popular. As expected this has resulted in an increase in online dating scams. It is now estimated that, in the UK alone, online dating scams are costing £24.5 million a year. British Police have received over 2,800 complaints of online dating scams.

Universal Scams & Fraud Detection

As with all cybercrime, the investigation and tracing of the criminals is both difficult and restrictive. Statistics indicates that the victims are typically aged between 40 and 59 with 64% of the complaints coming from females. Most perpetrators are known to be from Russia, Nigeria, Ghana, the UK and the USA.

In the United States the Federal Trade Commission reported receiving over 10,000 complaints of internet dating scams with victims being defrauded of an estimated €105 million. The FBI has a dedicated Internet Crimes Complaint Centre which pursues these criminals and provides advice on how we can learn to protect ourselves.

Men are not immune from internet dating fraud. In the UK 36% of all complaints to the police, come from men. Research would indicate, the most common cons on men is false advertisements posted by women supposedly looking to get married. Once the man contacts "the lady," the relationship develops quickly and, once it is established, the lady will advise that she is from a foreign country and will need money to cover her airfare and hotel if she is to visit him. Sometimes they advise that an independent travel agency will handle all of the flight bookings, paperwork and possible visa requirements. Once the deposit is made by the man, the supposed travel arrangements are made including the time and date of the flight arrival.

Internet Dating - Love Rats

However a short time before the proposed date of arrival, the lady will advise of an urgent problem, possibly health related or a relative having a problem. More money will be required to change the flight booking and then she will simply disappear.

LINDA'S STORY:

Linda is a 48 year old single mother living in Los Angeles. As a nurse, she works unsociable hours and decides to try internet dating. She is contacted by 'David', a charming man living in Abu Dhabi and they are soon emailing, talking on Skype and exchanging photographs. It wasn't long before David suggested moving to internet chat rooms, as it would be more private. Linda was swept away by his poetic words and kindness.

David tells Linda of his sick brother he cares for, telling her that, even if he could afford the airfare, he could not leave his brother to visit her in America. He also does not want her to visit him as he is embarrassed by his poor living conditions.

Besotted by David, Linda offers to pay not only for a nurse to care for his brother but also David's airfare to Los Angeles, a total of fourteen thousand dollars.

Linda who was now communicating with David for three months, transferred the money into a bank account provided by him. The money is taken from the account and she never hears from David again.

SANDRA'S STORY:

Sandra is a 57 year old widow living in Bristol, UK. Her husband left her with sufficient pension and life assurance to keep her comfortable for the rest of her life.

It was a friend who introduced her to online dating as she, the friend, had met a very nice man and was is a good relationship.

Sandra decides to try internet dating and it wasn't long before she had plenty of interest from many lonely hearted gentlemen, many widowed like herself. Unfortunately Sandra picked the black sheep amongst the flock of gentleman.

Jeff said that he was a successful entrepreneur in the oil business who made his money from dealing with the Arab nations, establishing contacts and negotiating deals. He was originally from Dallas Texas, had lived in London, but was now living in Warsaw Poland. Due to his business in the Middle-East, he spends a lot of time travelling between Asia and Europe. Sandra liked Jeff's profile and they started to communicate. After chatting online for a few months and swapping photographs, they finally agreed to meet in Paris, France, but the day before they were due to meet Jeff had to urgently fly to Malaysia to renegotiate a deal which had gone wrong.

The following day, Jeff contacts Sandra informing her of a major problem in Malaysia and that he needed £100,000 urgently to secure the multi-million dollar deal. Sandra, now smitten, offers him the money and is especially delighted when he promises her £500,000 as a return on her short term investment. But once the money was transferred, it and Jeff disappeared. Sandra was left shocked, heartbroken and broke. Just another statistic in the world of online dating scams.

Stephen's story:

Stephen is a gay man who lives in Chicago. A shy man, he doesn't like going to bars or clubs and instead he posts his profile on a gay dating website. Within a few days he starts chatting with Alex, who says he is based in Manchester, England. The online romance blossomed over the following two months, once again sharing photos and having regular chats on Skype.

Having proclaimed their love for each other, Stephen invited Alex to fly over to Chicago for a holiday. Alex agrees to visit Stephen after completing a month-long business trip to Thailand.

Universal Scams & Fraud Detection

While in Thailand, Alex told Stephen that he and his business have been robbed by a Thai gang He begged Stephen for help,. Stephen quickly transferred five thousand dollars to a bank account. Alex continues to ask for help, which, over a few weeks, results in Stephen giving Alex a total of US$450,000. When Stephen inevitably runs out of money, he soon finds that he can no longer contact Alex.

Both heartbroken and angry, Stephen tries to trace Alex and retains the services of a Private Investigator from the UK, who traced Alex to a company located in London with links to Africa. At the time of writing the British police are investigating this scam but, to date have been unable to recover Stephen's money.

Internet Dating - Love Rats

LESSONS LEARNED:

Users of online dating services should look out for the following warning signs:

- ✓ Declarations of love which come after an inappropriately short time of knowing the person
- ✓ The person claims to have a high-powered or glamorous job, especially if their work, 'takes them abroad a lot'
- ✓ Request for money at any time before meeting the person. Ideally no money should be exchanged before an actual relationship is established
- ✓ Photographs sent that are excessively glamorous and or possibly doctored to make the person appear more attractive. Genuine photographs may also have signs of dishonesty, such as wedding-ring marks
- ✓ Poor spelling and grammar, may indicate they are from a different country than advised
- ✓ Try to get you to move away from the dating site to other forms of internet chat rooms
- ✓ If you are concerned, ask them to send you a photo, clearly showing their face, whilst holding a newspaper of their location and displaying the date

Universal Scams & Fraud Detection

- ✓ If you do fall victim to online dating fraud, report it to your local law enforcement as soon as possible and try to preserve any evidence that maybe available on your computer.
- ✓ If it sounds too good to be true, it isn't true.

{18}

Fraud Terminology General Terms

Within the fraud investigation and law enforcement community, certain terminology is used to describe different aspects of fraud. For a person outside the community, or even for some persons within, the terminology can be confusing. Below is a list of words and phrases used by con artists and those trying to stop them. Of course, cons evolve, con artists adapt and prevention forces roll with new words.

Account takeover: This is a type of identity theft of an individual's bank account. The scam involves an identity thief taking control of the bank account of a victim, usually by obtaining an ATM card, a personal identification number (PIN) and / or bank account details. The con-artist furthers the fraud

Universal Scams & Fraud Detection

by contacting the bank and changing the mail addresses both physical and email for the posting of bank statements.

Application fraud: is when false information or failing to provide full information to a question at the application stage. It is most common in Mortgage fraud and at the policy completion stage of Insurance.

ATM Fraud: Automatic teller machine fraud involves the use of a bank card and pin number to obtain cash from a person's bank account. The bank card may have been skimmed and the pin number obtained by installing a small camera in the ATM.

Bank Fraud: The general term used in connection with committing fraud against a banking institution.

Backdoor: This is the term used for gaining remote access to a computer system without being detected.

Bin Raiding: is the searching through rubbish bins for information such as utility bills or bank statements which is then used by identity thefts for cloning your identity. A simple way of avoiding this fraud is by shredding all confidential information.

Card-Not-Present (CNP): When a Credit card is used to make a purchase and the card is not present for the transaction.

Fraud Terminology General Terms

An example of this would be booking airline tickets on the internet.

Cheque Fraud: The use of cheques for the purpose of fraud. This includes counterfeiting of cheques for financial gain.

Cybercrime: The terminology used to describe a crime using a computer and the internet.

Detection Rate: Most Special Investigation Units success is measured by detection rate and savings that is made from investigations.

Day of the Jackal Fraud: The theft of the identity of a baby, who was born around the same times as the perpetrator, whose birth was certified and who died shortly after. This is known as the "Day of the Jackal" fraud as its based on the famous book and movie of the same title.

Disruption: word used to describe the damage caused to a business from a successful fraud attack.

Encryption: The process of encoding electronic messages, files or other information in such a way that only authorised parties can access the data. It is not designed to prevent interception, but to deny access to the data content.

Universal Scams & Fraud Detection

Forgery: The act of falsely making or altering a document by which legal rights or obligations of another person are affected.

Fraudster: An individual who attempts to con another individual by way of committing a fraudulent act. A person cannot be called a fraudster until convicted in court.

Fraud Ring: This best describes a group of people whose aim is to work together to commit fraud against a financial institution or retail company.

Ghost Passenger: An individual falsely asserting, for the purpose of an insurance claim, to have been a passenger in a car involved in a traffic accident.

Ghost Insured: A motor insurance policy issued to a person who does not exist, or an individual using a false identity. After a short period of time an accident occurs involving the fake insured, crashing into a third party who sustains injury. When the investigator tries to locate the insured they have simply vanished, as if a Ghost.

Ghost Terminal: A credit card skimming machine that records your card details and your PIN number. It looks identical to a standard payment machine that you would see in a restaurant or retail outlet.

Fraud Terminology General Terms

Hacking: Gaining unauthorised access to computers which operate in a network.

Identity theft: The obtaining of an identity belonging to another person with the intention of causing deception for financial gain. The unauthorised use of a credit card belonging to another is considered identity theft.

Insurance Fraud (Claims): The false and/or gross exaggeration of a claim, which is known to be false, with the intent of deceiving the insurer to make a payment under a policy of insurance.

Internal Fraud: Fraud committed by an individual within a company or organisation, usually an employee or contractor.

Kiting Cheques: Using unauthorised credit to make a financial gain by way of deception with cheques. In theory a person will lodge a cheque into an account and then write a cheque from the account in which it is lodged, creating a false money float.

Lost Card Fraud: Using a credit card and then reporting it as being lost. This particular style of fraud has reduced since the establishment of using PIN numbers in Europe.

Malware: Computer software which has been developed for damaging computers. There are many different variants of Malware including Trojans, Viruses, Worms and spyware.

Universal Scams & Fraud Detection

Money Laundering: The process of taking the proceeds of criminal activity and making them appear legal.

Modus Operandi: A term used by law enforcement authorities, often abbreviated to 'M.O.', to describe the particular manner in which a crime is committed.

Nigerian Letter: Also known as the 419 letter scam. Once a common scam, most individuals and organisations are now aware of it. An individual is contacted, normally by email, by someone claiming to be a member of an African royal family. The person claims to have a large sum of money which they need to move out of the country and offer a large payment in return for use of a bank account to temporarily lodge the money. When the bank account details are sent, the account is emptied.

Phishing: The use of false emails or lies within emails for the purpose of obtaining confidential information such as dates of birth, credit card numbers or passwords.

Profiles: Credit Card owner information, which is held by the financial institution. It holds the general spending habits of the owner. Over a period of time the historical behaviours of the card holder are monitored for out of the ordinary or suspect transactions.

Fraud Terminology General Terms

Previous Address Fraud: When an individual moves from an address, a con artist uses an item of post, with the person's previous address to obtain their identity and pretends that the previous person is still living at the address. They then obtain credit and / or make purchases in that person's name.

Skimming: Reading the magnetic strip of a Credit Card with a magnetic reader, and using the information to create false credit cards.

Third Party Fraud: An individual that has had their identity stolen, is considered a third party. The fraudster is considered the first party and the financial institution the second party.

Theft: Property which is dishonestly taken from another, including deception, which permanently deprives the ownership and benefit to the rightful owner.

Epilogue.

In this book, I have done my utmost to provide the readers with facts, figures and case anecdotes which will enable them to gain knowledge of the different aspects of fraud and scams across the globe.

Fraud is not a unique crime, but many jurisdictions view fraud including cybercrime as a "soft" crime as, in the main, violence is not involved.

The development of new IT security systems enables co-operation and exchange of information between companies and financial institutions world-wide. But, what about individuals? The aftermath for a victim of fraud can be traumatic and leave them in a very vulnerable position.

Governments need to do more to recognise fraud against an individual or indeed, against an organisation and the associated costs, both personal and financial. Austerity measures and cuts in the budget of, for example, law enforcement agencies,

Universal Scams & Fraud Detection

materially hinders their work both in fraud protection and fraud detection. It is necessary for Governments to adequately fund such agencies and to work in harmony with industry organisations to identify and prevent fraudsters from plying their evil trade.

It is only by sharing criminal information and examining that information will we be in a position to join the dots, identify and prosecute fraudsters.

For now we must continue to work together, share our knowledge and experience, united as citizens and organisations in the prevention of crime.

Thank you,
David Snow.

About the Author

David Snow lives in Dublin Ireland, with his wife Jacinta and three daughters Kirsten, Olivia and Sarah.

For further information, including TV and radio interviews please view his website, link below.

Also available by the Author

Someone Has Taken My Place – Paperback and Kindle format

www.davidsnow.ie or www.davidsnowauthor.com